DUTY and GLORY

EUROPE
1660–1698

CW00922414

Written by Nik Gaukroger and
Richard Bodley Scott, assisted by
Paul Robinson, John Munro, Mike Kroon,
David Cáceres Gallardo and Karsten Loh

OSPREY
PUBLISHING

SLITHERINE

First published in Great Britain in 2011 by Osprey Publishing Ltd.

© 2011 Osprey Publishing Ltd and Slitherine Software UK Ltd.

Osprey Publishing
Midland House, West Way, Botley, Oxford OX2 0PH, UK
44–02 23rd St, Suite 219, Long Island City, NY 11101, USA
E-mail: info@ospreypublishing.com

Slitherine Software UK Ltd
The White Cottage, 8 West Hill Avenue, Epsom, KT19 8LE, UK
E-mail: info@slitherine.co.uk

All rights reserved. Apart from any fair dealing for the purpose
of private study, research, criticism or review, as permitted under
the Copyright, Designs and Patents Act, 1988, no part of this
publication may be reproduced, stored in a retrieval system, or
transmitted in any form or by any means, electronic, electrical,
chemical, mechanical, optical, photocopying, recording or otherwise,
without the prior written permission of the copyright owner.
Enquiries should be addressed to the Publishers.

A CIP catalogue record for this book is available from the
British Library

ISBN: 978 1 84908 233 4
E-book ISBN: 978 1 84908 234 1

Cover concept and page layout by Myriam Bell Design, France
Typeset in Adobe Caslon Pro
Cover artwork by Peter Dennis

Photography supplied by Front Rank Figurines, Legio Heroica,
Sergei Sharenko, Simon Clarke, Juergen Mueller, Old Glory, Reiver
Castings/Northumbria Painting Services

Project management by JD McNeil and Osprey Team
Technical management by Iain McNeil
Index by Michael Forder
Originated by PDQ Media, Bungay, UK
Printed in China through Worldprint Ltd

11 12 13 14 15   10 9 8 7 6 5 4 3 2 1

Osprey Publishing is supporting the Woodland Trust, the UK's
leading woodland conservation charity, by funding the dedication
of trees.

www.ospreypublishing.com
www.slitherine.com

CONTENTS

INTRODUCTION

The fifty years that followed the end of the Thirty Years' War in 1648 were mostly dominated, in Western Europe, by the ambitions and actions of one man, Louis XIV of France, and his influence was felt in Eastern Europe at times as well. From 1667 Louis engaged in a series of wars against his neighbours which, depending on perspective, were either aggressive land grabs, or wars to secure the natural frontiers of France against the hostile nations who virtually surrounded it on all sides. What is certain is that Louis was not reluctant to use military force to further his aims. Having *Ultima Ratio Regum* ("last argument of kings") cast on the barrels of his cannon is a good indication of this. He is reputed to have admitted on his death bed that, perhaps, he had "loved war too much", which would be scant consolation to those who had suffered and died in the conflicts he started.

The general battle order of Western European armies during this period continued as before, with an infantry centre and mounted wings, each typically in two or more lines. However, there were important changes in the infantry arm. The primacy of the musket as the infantry weapon of choice was confirmed once and for all. The invention of the bayonet presaged the end of the usefulness of the pike, as the musketeer could now also be his own pikeman – a universal infantryman. Initially, the bayonet was the "plug" variety which was, to all intents, a long dagger pushed into the end of the musket to create a spear with which he could hold off cavalry. Obviously this had the drawback that whilst the bayonet was in use the musket could not be fired. Thus at this stage the gain was limited and the pike remained in use, although in declining numbers, and indeed some

armies did go so far as to discard it well before the end of the period. The real breakthrough came with the invention of the "socket" bayonet, sometimes attributed to the great French siege engineer, Vauban. This allowed the bayonet to be fixed in place by means of a ring-shaped socket which went over the barrel, thus allowing the musket to be fired even when the bayonet was fixed. This allowed the musketeer to both shoot and act as a spearman at need. This finally killed off the pike as a useful battlefield weapon.

The musket itself evolved during this period. At the end of the Thirty Years' War the vast majority of infantry firearms were matchlock muskets, using a lighted cord, or match, to ignite the pan of powder to fire the musket. This clearly had a number of disadvantages, one of which being that during the loading process the musketeer had to both hold this lighted match and pour gunpowder into his musket at the same time – in the stressful heat of battle it was all too possible for this to go wrong with explosive results. Additionally, there are a number of cases of excited soldiers collecting extra powder from regimental barrels behind the lines forgetting to put down their match before reaching in. Couple this with the carrying of charges of gunpowder in bandoliers around the body (the so called twelve apostles) and musketeer formations had to have relatively wide spacing between the men to minimise the risk of accidents. This lessened the effects of musketry on opposing formations. As the period progressed, more and more armies started to replace the matchlock with various varieties of flintlock muskets, which did not need a lighted match to ignite the powder charge. Whilst this allowed the musket to be loaded a little faster, the main benefit to begin with

Dumbarton's Regiment of Foot

was safety, and the removal of the logistical burden of supplying large numbers of musketeers with match cord - which literally went up in flames while in use, even during periods of waiting for action. By the end of the century, the near universal use of prepared cartridges, and the development of new firing methods, allowed musketeers to be placed closer together to deliver more concentrated and rapid fire to greater effect. The full impact of these changes, however, were really only felt in the succeeding century.

Cavalry warfare in this period remained, in Western Europe, more or less unchanged from how it had been at the end of the Thirty Years' War, and "horse" still formed about 30 percent of the armies of the major states. The biggest change appears to have been the discarding of body armour by the cavalry of many armies with, at most, a buff coat remaining. The three-quarter armoured cuirassier was now very much a thing of the past.

Western European warfare of this period was often dominated by sieges and manoeuvre rather than decisive pitched battles. Thus, whilst the major encounters of the time were often hard fought and bloody affairs, they rarely led to large-scale gains for the winners either militarily or politically, as the defeated party usually had defensive positions that allowed them time to regroup and rebuild their forces. Warfare was highly attritional, with vast numbers of men and horses being fielded at huge expense to their masters. For example, in the War of the League of Augsburg, the French had, in theory, over 420,000 men under arms, more than would be fielded in the following War of the Spanish Succession. The impact of these armies on the areas they operated in was high. Just as in the Thirty Years' War, armies lived off the local population through the "contributions" system, which was in effect a tax by the army on the locals, be they friendly or hostile.

In Eastern Europe the major powers at the start of the period were the Polish-Lithuanian Commonwealth and Sweden, the latter emerging from the Thirty Years' War as a perhaps unlikely superpower. Sweden was in a slightly difficult situation. Although a major military power, with a large and effective army often containing many mercenaries, it was not able to fully support its military machine from its own resources, and thus tended to rely on large financial subsidies from its French ally. This reduced its scope for politically independent action. Any wars had to be paid for by allies, or by the enemy through the army supplying itself from enemy lands. The "sleeping giant" of Russia was starting to stir during this period, and flexed its military muscles at the expense of the Commonwealth in the west and the Tatars in the east. However, it was to be in the 18th century, under Peter the Great, that Russia truly came to the fore as a great power.

Possibly the biggest winners in Eastern Europe in the second half of the 17th century were the Austrians. With their political ambitions in Germany curbed by the terms of the Peace of Westphalia in 1648, their attention shifted eastwards instead. With the defeat of the Turks in 1664 and, most famously, in 1683, although in both cases the Austrians needed significant foreign assistance, it became clear that the Turks had finally run out of steam, and that the reconquest of Ottoman Hungary and neighbouring lands was a real possibility. By the end of the century Austria had made enough gains that it was actually able to fight a war against the Turks in the east whilst intervening effectively in Western Europe as well.

Warfare in the east remained a more mobile affair than in the west, with larger distances to be covered and large open plains in many areas. Thus in many armies cavalry retained its primacy, although both the Russians and the Polish-Lithuanian Commonwealth recognised the usefulness of solid infantry, and raised large numbers of Western European-style units, usually trained by veterans of western conflicts. Even the cavalry in the east began to change, with Western European-style horsemen becoming more and more common, either as mercenaries or as a result of "native" units being "modernised". Russia was especially influenced by Western European military equipment and organisation, the Poles less so, with more traditional types actually seeing a resurgence at the end of the century.

Polish Pancerni

LATER RUSSIAN

This list covers Russian armies from 1630, when native Russians in western-style units were introduced by Tsar Mikhail Romanov, until 1698.

The first test of the new regiments came in 1632, when the Tsar sent an army into the territory of the Polish-Lithuanian Commonwealth to retake the strategic city of Smolensk, which Russia had been forced to cede in 1618. Despite the new troops, and a massive superiority in the number of soldiers available at the start of the war, the Russians were unable to properly concentrate their impressive siege train, and the siege of Smolensk dragged on into 1633. This gave the Poles time to raise relief forces and to cut the besiegers' lines of supply, which forced the Russians to surrender in early 1634. It should be noted, however, that the new Russian army performed much better in actions away from Smolensk.

Russia's next major enterprise was the Thirteen Years' War between 1654 and 1667, once again against the Commonwealth. With the Poles fighting against a Cossack rebellion, which itself had Russian support, the time seemed ripe for another attempt at making gains at the expense of the Poles. In 1654 the Russians crossed the border and again besieged Smolensk, this time successfully, defeating a Polish relief army along the way. Russian progress was assisted by the entry of Sweden into the war in 1655. Faced with two opponents, Polish resistance all but collapsed, with large parts of the country over-run by enemies. However, the Poles showed their mettle and, setting aside their differences and regrouping, they counter-attacked and drove the invaders back from a large part of their conquests. Russia was now drawn into the debilitating conflict involving the Cossacks in the Ukraine, which distracted them from finishing off their conquests in Poland and Lithuania proper. Driven back to their own territory by 1664, the Russians were again aided by a civil war in the Commonwealth and, with the threat of an Ottoman invasion, peace was agreed in 1667 following three years of negotiations. By the terms of the peace, Russia finally regained Smolensk along with additional territory.

For the rest of the century Russia's wars were to be in the east against the Turks. The first conflict, 1676–81, was caused by the Turks attempting to gain control of the territories on the right bank of the Dnieper in the Ukraine. The main fighting was over the town of Chyhyryn. The Turks failed to capture this in 1677, with their besieging army roughly handled by the Russian relieving forces, but they returned the next year and succeeded in capturing the town despite the Russians breaking through their covering army. The rest of the war saw the Russians fighting off repeated attacks by the Ottomans' Crimean Tatar allies.

War resumed again as the Russians joined the anti-Ottoman coalition that was created following the Turkish repulse from Vienna in 1683. Initially the Russians concentrated on the Crimea, campaigning there in 1687 and 1689, with the aim of subduing the Ottomans' loyal, and dangerous, Tatar allies. Large numbers of Cossacks joined the campaigns. Previous Russian campaigns in the Crimea in the preceding century had failed due to a breakdown in logistics, the Russians being unable to supply large forces across the steppe. Although they had somewhat improved their logistics in the 17th century, the Russians once again failed to be able to fully supply their troops in the far south, meaning that they could not undertake the necessary sieges to break Tatar power. However, in terms of the wider conflict, the campaigns did draw off some Ottoman forces and tie down the Tatars.

The last Russian campaigns of this period were also the first conducted by Peter the Great, and were directed at Azov during 1695–96. To avoid the problems of supply across the vast steppe, Peter chose to move along the Don River so that he could supply the army from boats. The first attempt was a failure, as the Russians could not control the river, but the following year, with a flotilla built for the purpose, they were able to do so, seeing off a Turkish fleet. Azov then surrendered after a massive bombardment and a Cossack assault.

TROOP NOTES

Russian cavalry raised by the traditional *pomest'e* system retained the horse archer tactics that they had adopted centuries earlier under Mongol influence. Whilst the ideal was for the rider to be well-armoured, many made do with quilted armour, especially the less well-off. During this period the quality, and quantity, of this cavalry declined dramatically as western-style cavalry, known as *reitary*, were preferred. Indeed, many who would previously have served in traditional cavalry formations now served in reitary ones. From 1662 the pomest'e cavalry were not always called upon to serve in the field.

Russian reitary regiments were larger than contemporary western cavalry units, but were equipped and fought in a western manner.

Streltsy were professional infantry founded by Ivan IV in 1550 to provide the Russian army with a reliable infantry force. They were armed with long firearms and a heavy berdische axe, which could also be used as a rest for the firearm. The streltsy were so useful that their numbers rapidly increased, and they were deployed as garrisons throughout Russia, however over time their quality deteriorated, especially as the importance of the western-style *soldaty* increased.

From 1630, increasing use was made of native Russian infantry, known as *soldaty*, organised into western-style units trained by experienced foreign officers who had learnt their trade in the Thirty Years' War and similar conflicts. The soldaty were recruited by conscription on an annual basis, and many units were only in being for part of the year, being disbanded over the winter months. Despite this "part time" basis, the soldaty proved to be a useful resource and acted as a counter balance to the existing streltsy. From 1689, following campaigns in the Crimea, the soldaty regiments were more or less disbanded on a permanent basis, with only two remaining in being in 1694, which resulted in them being of poor quality when they were reformed when needed.

In 1683 the then 10-year-old Tsar Peter formed a "play" army at the royal lodge at Preobrazhenskoe. By 1687, with drafts of streltsy volunteers, these numbered 600 and were split into the *Preobrazhenski* and *Semenovski* companies, which went on to form the nucleus of Peter's life guard regiments of the same names in 1695. Peter's wargames with his "play" army, and regular troops drafted in to provide opposition, were serious affairs, sometimes with significant casualties, and on one occasion the Tsar himself was wounded.

Traditional Russian Cavalry

LATER RUSSIAN

LATER RUSSIAN STARTER ARMY (FROM 1662)		
Commander-in-Chief	1	Field Commander
Sub-Commanders	2	2 x Troop Commander
Traditional cavalry	1 BG	4 bases of Traditional cavalry: Average, Unarmoured Cavalry – Bow, Swordsmen
Reitary	2 BGs	Each comprising 4 bases of Reitary: Average, Armoured Determined Horse – Impact Pistol, Melee Pistol
Reitary	1 BG	4 bases of Reitary: Average, Unarmoured Determined Horse – Impact Pistol, Melee Pistol
Cossack cavalry	1 BG	4 bases of Average, Unarmoured Light Horse – Carbine, Light Lancers, Melee Pistol
Streltsy	1 BG	8 bases of Streltsy: Average, Unarmoured Medium Foot – Musket, Heavy Weapon
Soldaty	2 BGs	Each comprising 6 bases of Soldaty: 4 bases of Average, Unarmoured Medium Foot – Musket; and 2 bases of Average, Unarmoured Heavy Foot – Pike
Dragoons	1 BG	4 bases of Dragoons: Average, Unarmoured Dragoons – Musket
Nariad	1 BG	2 bases of Nariad – Average Heavy Artillery
Camp	1	Unfortified camp
Total	10 BGs	Camp, 20 mounted bases, 26 foot bases, 3 commanders

Muscovy Strelets, 1670, by Angus McBride © Osprey Publishing Ltd.
Taken from Men-at-Arms 427: Armies of Ivan the Terrible.

BUILDING A CUSTOMISED LIST USING OUR ARMY POINTS

Choose an army based on the maxima and minima in the list below. The following special instructions apply to this army:

- Commanders should be depicted as traditional cavalry or reitary.

- The minimum marked * only applies before 1662.
- The minimum marked ** only applies from 1662.
- Lancers and Hussars cannot be fielded together.
- From 1690 a maximum of 2 battle groups of Average Soldaty can be fielded.

LATER RUSSIAN									
Territory Types: Agricultural, Steppes									
C-in-C		Great Commander/Field Commander/Troop Commander				80/50/35		1	
Sub-commanders		Field Commander				50		0–2	
		Troop Commander				35		0–3	
Troop name		Troop Type			Capabilities			Points per base	Bases per BG	Total bases
		Type	Armour	Quality	Shooting	Impact	Melee			
Core Troops										
Traditional cavalry	Only before 1662	Cavalry	Armoured	Superior	Bow	–	Swordsmen	16	4–6	0–12	*8–32
				Average				12		
	Any date	Cavalry	Unarmoured	Average	Bow	–	Swordsmen	10	4–6	0–32
				Poor				8		
Reitary	Any date	Horse	Armoured	Average	Carbine		Pistol	11	4–6	0–12
				Poor				8		
		Horse	Unarmoured	Average	Carbine		Pistol	9	4–6	
				Poor				7		
	Only from 1635 to 1661	Horse	Armoured	Average	–	Pistol	Pistol	10	4–6	4–16	**8–30
				Poor				7		
		Horse	Unarmoured	Average	–	Pistol	Pistol	8	4–6	
				Poor				6		
	Only from 1662	Determined Horse	Armoured	Average	–	Pistol	Pistol	15	4–6	4–24
		Determined Horse	Unarmoured	Average	–	Pistol	Pistol	12	4–6	
				Poor				9		
Dragoons		Dragoons	Unarmoured	Average	Musket	–	–	8	3 or 4	0–4 before 1642, 0–12 from 1642
Streltsy		Medium Foot	Unarmoured	Average	Musket	Heavy Weapon	Heavy Weapon	8	6–8	6–48 before 1662
		Medium Foot	Unarmoured	Poor	Musket	Heavy Weapon	Heavy Weapon	6	6–8	6–24 from 1662
Soldaty		Medium Foot	Unarmoured	Average	Musket	–	–	8	4	6	6–60
		Heavy Foot	Unarmoured	Average	–	Pike	Pike	5	2	
		Medium Foot	Unarmoured	Poor	Musket	–	–	6	4	6
		Heavy Foot	Unarmoured	Poor	–	Pike	Pike	3	2	
Nariad		Heavy Artillery	–	Average	Heavy Artillery	–	–	25	2, 3 or 4	2–4
		Medium Artillery	–	Average	Medium Artillery	–	–	20	2, 3 or 4	

Optional Troops										
Tatar or Kalmyk cavalry		Light Horse	Unarmoured	Average	Bow	–	Swordsmen	9	4–6	0–8
		Cavalry	Unarmoured	Average	Bow	–	Swordsmen	10	4–6	
Cossack infantry	Only before 1650	Medium Foot	Unarmoured	Average	Arquebus	–	–	6	6–8	0–24
	Any date	Medium Foot	Unarmoured	Average	Musket	–	–	7	6–8	
Cossack cavalry	Any date	Light Horse	Unarmoured	Average	Carbine	Light Lancers	Swordsmen	10	4–6	0–12
		Cavalry	Unarmoured	Average	Carbine	–	Swordsmen	10	4–6	
		Cavalry	Unarmoured	Average	–	Light Lancers	Swordsmen	9	4–6	
	Only from 1650	Light horse	Unarmoured	Average	Carbine	Light Lancers	Pistol	10	4–6	
		Cavalry	Unarmoured	Average	Carbine	–	Pistol	10	4–6	
		Cavalry	Unarmoured	Average	–	Light Lancers	Pistol	9	4–6	
Provincial musketeers, pribory		Medium Foot	Unarmoured	Poor	Musket	–	–	5	6–8	0–16
Lancers	Only from 1662	Cavalry	Armoured	Average	–	Light Lancers	Swordsmen	11	4–6	0–6
Hussars		Determined Horse	Armoured	Average	–	Light Lancers	Pistol	15	4	0–4
Peter the Great's guard infantry	Only from 1695	Medium Foot	Unarmoured	Superior	Musket	Bayonet	Bayonet	11	5	6	0–6
		Heavy Foot	Unarmoured	Superior	–	Pike	Pike	8	1	
Sorokas, valkoneyka and other light guns		Light Artillery	–	Average	Light Artillery	–	–	12	2, 3 or 4	0–4
Gulay gorod		Field Fortifications	–	–	–	–	–	3	–	0–16
Fortified camp								24		0–1

LATER POLISH AND LITHUANIAN

This list covers Polish/Lithuanian armies from 1632 to 1698.

This period opened for the Polish-Lithuanian Commonwealth with a short, sharp war with Russia over possession of Smolensk. Despite being rather unprepared for the war, and unable to prevent the Russians from besieging the city, the garrison held out bravely for over a year, during which time the Poles raised armies to cut the Russian supply lines and force their ignominious surrender in 1634. At the same time they had to repel a serious Tatar invasion, which led to a Polish incursion onto Ottoman territory. However, a full scale war with the Turks was avoided.

Polish Winged Hussar

The next major conflict that engulfed the Commonwealth, and threatened its very existence, has become known as "The Deluge", for the scale and suddenness of its hardships. The emergency began with an uprising of Cossacks in Ukraine in 1648, resulting in independence for the Cossacks around Kiev, despite the Poles' attempts to subdue them by force. Following this, the Cossacks concluded the Treaty of Pereyaslav with Russia. This gave the Tsar the opportunity he had been waiting for to invade in 1654, and Russian armies overran the entire eastern part of Poland. Taking advantage of Poland's preoccupation with the Cossacks and the Russians, Karl X of Sweden opportunistically intervened the following year. Most of the Polish nobility, along with Frederick William of Brandenburg-Prussia, agreed to recognize Karl as King of Poland after he promised to drive out the Russians. However, the Swedish armies instead ravaged the countryside, which caused the Polish populace to rise up in revolt. Despite this, the Swedes overran the remainder of Poland except for Lvov and Danzig.

Despite these almost insurmountable difficulties, the Poles rallied and fought back, managing to recover most of their lost territory from the Swedes.

Polish Commander

In exchange for breaking the alliance with Sweden, Frederick William, in his capacity as the ruler of Ducal Prussia, was released from his vassalage to the Polish crown and abandoned his alliance with the Swedes. The Poles were now in the ascendant, with much of the occupied part of the country in open revolt against Karl. He, when presented with the opportunity to leave Poland to invade Denmark, who had declared war on him, took it with alacrity as a face-saving way of abandoning his conquests without further fighting. The Commonwealth could now turn to removing the Russians and reclaiming their land, which they all but managed by 1664. However, internal conflict meant that when peace was agreed in 1667 they had to cede Smolensk and the easternmost third of Ukraine. For the best part of the next decade, until Jan III Sobieski assumed the throne in 1674, the Commonwealth remained in turmoil.

Sobieski clearly decided that the best way to reunite the country was to go to war with the Turks, no doubt hoping that it would take on some aspects of a crusade. A short war between 1674 and 1676 achieved very little, but it did establish Sobieski's authority, and in the following years he was able to re-impose royal power over the Commonwealth. His greatest moment came in 1683 when the Turks, following a 20 year truce, once again invaded Austria with the aim of capturing Vienna. Whilst the siege was in progress, an allied army made up of Austrian, German and Polish troops, under the banner of a Holy League, was assembled to relieve the city and drive the Turks back into Hungary. Sobieski was appointed commander of the combined army and, on 12 September 1683, won a great victory outside the walls of Vienna, leading the final decisive charge of the Polish hussars personally. A few weeks later he won another victory over the retreating Turks at the Battle of Párkány, with the Polish cavalry again delivering the decisive charge to break the Ottomans.

TROOP NOTES

Each hussar company (*rota*) was commanded by a *rotmistrz* who commissioned wealthy men known as *towarzysze* ("companions") to raise a number of cavalry in a manner similar to the old medieval lance. The towarzysze would recruit retainers (*pacholiks*) to make up the number of soldiers required. There could be as many as 7 of these. The towarzysze were splendidly equipped, as befitted wealthy men in a society that prized ostentatious displays of personal wealth, and it is from their equipment that we have our image of the hussars at their height. However, the pacholiks would be less well-equipped, and certainly less dramatically. Whilst the armour of the best-equipped would justify Heavily Armoured classification, the majority of the hussars were not equipped to that standard, and so we classify the battle groups as Armoured.

The hussar's main weapon was the 5-metre *kopia* lance, which was hollow and made from cheap wood. As this would inevitably shatter on impact, the hussar carried a long heavy sword, called a *koncerz*, as a back-up to be used in a lance-like manner in subsequent charges. In a hard-fought battle it was seen as a dishonourable thing not to have shattered your kopia, as this meant you had not been in the thick of the fighting. The hussars also carried a pair of pistols, and many pacholiks were issued with an arquebus or similar. However, these were very much secondary weapons, even after the lance had been broken, when the rider's sabre, called a *pallash*, was the favoured weapon.

Despite their continued effectiveness on the battlefield, the number of hussars fielded in this period, especially between 1652 and 1662, was much lower than had been the case in earlier decades. The majority of Polish mounted were now the Cossack-style cavalry who had previously supported the hussars. The armoured Cossacks were, from 1648 or so, referred to as *pancerni*, and became the most numerous of the Polish cavalry. Their primary weapons were initially firearms, both carbines and pistols, but from 1676 most

Polish Infantry

were armed with a light lance and were used as shock cavalry in support of, and to some extent replacing, the hussars.

Skirmishing light cavalry was now mainly supplied by so called "Tatars" and "Wallachians", although these terms had little to do with ethnicity, but instead was a reference to their dress, which had been adopted from these peoples. The Cossacks now only supplied heavier types of cavalry. Whilst the "Tatars" continued to disdain the use of firearms, the "Wallachians" started to adopt them.

German cavalry, known as *raytars*, were used in numbers during this period, and at times even outnumbered the hussars. By the later 17th century they had become known as *arkebusiers*.

Infantry were now more important in Polish armies, sometimes contributing over half the army.

The mainstay of the foot were infantry regiments organised, equipped and dressed in contemporary German style, trained by experienced mercenaries. Initially many were also comprised of foreigners, although the demands of the Thirty Years' War limited their availability. However, they were soon made up of mostly native Poles. Light battalion guns were sometimes attached to infantry units from about 1552 to 1662, but this practice was not continued thereafter and these guns were instead deployed in separate batteries.

From about 1673, infantry regiments were reformed, with the number of pikemen being reduced to roughly 10 percent of the total and their pikes shortened, and the musketeers being armed with the berdische axe. They also adopted Polish-style dress. By the siege of Vienna in 1683, the reforms appear to have been complete.

LATER POLISH AND LITHUANIAN STARTER ARMY (1676-1679)		
Commander-in-Chief	1	Field Commander
Sub-Commanders	2	2 x Troop Commander
Hussars	1 BG	4 bases of Hussars: Superior, Armoured Determined Horse – Impact Mounted, Swordsmen
Armoured Cossacks or pancerni	1 BG	4 bases of Armoured Cossacks or pancerni: Superior, Armoured Cavalry – Light Lancers, Melee Pistol
Other Cossacks	1 BG	4 bases of Other Cossacks: Average, Unarmoured Cavalry – Carbine, Swordsmen
German raytars	1 BG	4 bases of German raytars: Average, Unarmoured Determined Horse – Impact Pistol, Melee Pistol
"Tatar" or "Wallachian" light cavalry	1 BG	4 bases of "Tatar" or "Wallachian" light cavalry: Average, Unarmoured Light Horse – Bow, Swordsmen
"German"-style infantry regiments	2 BGs	Each comprising 6 bases of "German"-style infantry regiments: 4 bases of Average, Unarmoured Medium Foot – Musket; and 2 bases of Average, Unarmoured Heavy Foot – Pike
Haiduks and registered Cossacks	2 BGs	Each comprising 6 bases of Haiduks and registered Cossacks: Average, Unarmoured Medium Foot – Musket
Fake hussars	1 BG	4 bases of Poor, Unarmoured Mob
Dragoons	1 BG	3 bases of Dragoons: Average, Unarmoured Dragoons – Musket
Camp	1	Unfortified camp
Total	11 BGs	Camp, 20 mounted bases, 31 foot bases, 3 commanders

BUILDING A CUSTOMISED LIST USING OUR ARMY POINTS

Choose an army based on the maxima and minima in the list below. The following special instructions apply to this army:

- Commanders should be depicted as hussars.
- Players using fake hussars can deploy hussar bases, which must be replaced by bases depicting mob or peasants on poor mounts as soon as enemy within 6 MUs can see them. They can be deployed within 12 MUs of a side table edge as if mounted troops. In all other respects they are treated as normal Mob.
- There must be at least as many Cossack, pancerni or petyhortsy battle groups fielded as there are hussar battle groups.
- From 1652 to 1662 there must be at least as many raytar bases as hussar bases.
- As usual, Regimental Guns must be the same quality as the battle group.

Polish Hussar, 1672–83, by Angus McBride © Osprey Publishing Ltd. Taken from Men-at-Arms 184: Polish Armies 1569–1696 (1).

LATER POLISH AND LITHUANIAN

Territory Types: Agricultural, Woodlands, Steppes

C-in-C		Great Commander/Field Commander/Troop Commander						80/50/35	1	
Sub-commanders		Field Commander						50	0–2	
		Troop Commander						35	0–3	
Troop name		**Troop Type**			**Capabilities**			**Points per base**	**Bases per BG**	**Total bases**
		Type	Armour	Quality	Shooting	Impact	Melee			
Core Troops										
Hussars		Determined Horse	Armoured	Superior	–	Impact Mounted	Swordsmen	23	4–6	4–16
Armoured Cossacks or pancerni	Only before 1676	Cavalry	Armoured	Superior / Average	Carbine	–	Pistol	16 / 12	4–6	4–36
	Only from 1676	Cavalry	Armoured	Superior / Average	–	Light Lancers	Pistol	15 / 11	4–6	
Lithuanian petyhortsy		Cavalry	Armoured / Unarmoured	Average	Bow*	Light Lancers	Swordsmen	12 / 10	4–6	
Other Cossacks		Cavalry	Unarmoured	Average	Carbine	–	Swordsmen	10	4–6	
		Cavalry	Unarmoured	Average	Bow	–	Swordsmen	10	4–6	
German raytars or "arkebusiers"	Only before 1650	Horse	Armoured	Average / Poor	–	Pistol	Pistol	10 / 7	4	4–12
		Horse	Unarmoured	Average / Poor	–	Pistol	Pistol	8 / 6	4	
	Only from 1640	Determined Horse	Armoured	Average / Poor	–	Pistol	Pistol	15 / 11	4	
		Determined Horse	Unarmoured	Average / Poor	–	Pistol	Pistol	12 / 9	4	
"German"-style infantry regiments	Only before 1680	Medium Foot	Unarmoured	Average	Musket	–	–	8	4 } 6	6–48
		Heavy Foot	Unarmoured	Average	–	Pike	Pike	5	2	
		Medium Foot	Unarmoured	Poor	Musket	–	–	6	4 } 6	
		Heavy Foot	Unarmoured	Poor	–	Pike	Pike	3	2	
Polish-style infantry regiments	Only from 1673	Medium Foot	Unarmoured	Average / Poor	Musket	Heavy Weapon	Heavy Weapon	8 / 6	6	
Light guns attached to infantry regiments	Only from 1652 to 1662	Regimental Guns	–	Average / Poor	Regimental Guns	Regimental Guns	–	9 / 7	n/a	0–1 per "German"-style infantry regiments BG
Artillery		Medium Artillery	–	Average	Medium Artillery	–	–	20	2	0–2 } 0–4
		Light Artillery	–	Average	Light Artillery	–	–	12	2, 3 or 4	0–4
Optional Troops										
"Tatar" or "Wallachian" light cavalry		Light Horse	Unarmoured	Average	Bow	–	Swordsmen	9	4–6	0–24 } 0–24
		Light Horse	Unarmoured	Average	Carbine	–	Swordsmen	9	4–6	0–12
Haiduks and registered Cossacks	Only before 1665	Medium Foot	Unarmoured	Average	Musket	–	Swordsmen	8	6–8	0–12
	Any date	Medium Foot	Unarmoured	Average	Musket	–	–	7	6–8	
Noble levy		Cavalry	Armoured	Poor	Bow	–	–	7	8–10	0–20
Dragoons and cossacks		Dragoons	Unarmoured	Average	Musket	–	–	8	3 or 4	0–8
Peasant infantry		Mob	Unarmoured	Poor	–	–	–	2	8–12	0–12
Fake hussars		Mob	Unarmoured	Poor	–	–	–	2	4–6	0–6

LATER POLISH AND LITHUANIAN

"Janissary" and other guards	Only from 1673	Medium Foot	Unarmoured	Superior	Musket	–	Swordsmen	11	4	0–4
Tabor wagon laager	Field Fortifications	–	–	–	–	–		3	–	0–12
Fortified camp	–	–	–	–	–	–		24	–	0–1
Allies										
Ukrainian Cossack allies (Only before 1648 or after 1657) – Cossack – see FOGR Companion 3: *Clash of Empires*										
Crimean Tatar allies (Only from 1655) – Tatar – see FOGR Companion 3: *Clash of Empires*										

LATER POLISH AND LITHUANIAN ALLIES

Allied commander		Field Commander/Troop Commander						40/25	1	
Troop name		**Troop Type**			**Capabilities**			**Points per base**	**Bases per BG**	**Total bases**
		Type	Armour	Quality	Shooting	Impact	Melee			
Hussars		Determined Horse	Armoured	Superior	–	Impact Mounted	Swordsmen	23	4–6	4–8
Armoured Cossacks or pancerni	Only before 1576	Cavalry	Armoured	Superior	Carbine	–	Pistol	16	4–6	4–12
				Average				12		
	Only from 1576	Cavalry	Armoured	Superior	–	Light Lancers	Pistol	15	4–6	
				Average				11		
Lithuanian petyhortsy		Cavalry	Armoured	Average	Bow*	Light Lancers	Swordsmen	12	4–6	
			Unarmoured					10		
Other Cossacks		Cavalry	Unarmoured	Average	Carbine	–	Swordsmen	10	4–6	
		Cavalry	Unarmoured	Average	Bow	–	Swordsmen	10	4–6	
German "raytars"	Only before 1650	Horse	Armoured	Average	–	Pistol	Pistol	10	4	0–8
				Poor				7		
		Horse	Unarmoured	Average	–	Pistol	Pistol	8	4	
				Poor				6		
	Only from 1640	Determined Horse	Armoured	Average	–	Pistol	Pistol	15	4	
				Poor				11		
		Determined Horse	Unarmoured	Average	–	Pistol	Pistol	12	4	
				Poor				9		
"German"-style infantry regiments	Only before 1680	Medium Foot	Unarmoured	Average	Musket	–	–	8	4	6	0–18
		Heavy Foot	Unarmoured	Average	–	Pike	Pike	5	2	
		Medium Foot	Unarmoured	Poor	Musket	–	–	6	4	6
		Heavy Foot	Unarmoured	Poor	–	Pike	Pike	3	2	
Polish-style infantry regiments	Only from 1673	Medium Foot	Unarmoured	Average	Musket	Heavy Weapon	Heavy Weapon	8	6	
				Poor				6		
Light guns attached to infantry regiments	Only from 1652 to 1662	Regimental Guns	–	Average	Regimental Guns	Regimental Guns	–	9	n/a	0–1 per "German"-style infantry regiments BG
				Poor				7		
Artillery		Medium Artillery	–	Average	Medium Artillery	–	–	20	2	0–2
		Light Artillery	–	Average	Light Artillery	–	–	12	2	

Polish Infantry at Vienna, 1683, by Angus McBride © Osprey Publishing Ltd. Taken from Men-at-Arms 188: Polish Armies 1569–1696 (2).

LATER VENETIAN COLONIAL

*T*his list covers the armies of the Venetian Republic that fought overseas from 1645 until 1698.

After decades of relatively peaceful co-existence, if we ignore the endemic piracy in the eastern Mediterranean, in 1645 the Venetians once again found themselves at war with the Ottoman Turks when the latter invaded the Venetian coastal possessions in Dalmatia and the island of Crete. The ensuing war, which lasted until 1669, is known as the War of Candia or the Cretan War.

By fooling the Venetians into thinking that they were going to attack Malta, the Ottomans took the Venetians by surprise when instead they landed on Crete in June 1645. The island's defences were in a poor state, despite some attempts to improve them the previous year, and the Turks quickly took a number of towns and fortresses, including the second city of the island, Canea. A Venetian naval counter-attack later in the year failed to retake the city. By 1648 all of Crete apart from Candia, and a few outlying fortresses, were in Ottoman hands.

The ensuing siege lasted until 1669, with the Venetians surviving only thanks to their navy, which could get supplies into the city and, to distract the Ottoman navy, also conducted operations in the Dardanelles to disrupt the Turkish supply lines. During this time the Venetians received direct military aid from the French, both naval and land troops. However, these were withdrawn in 1669, leaving the garrison in an untenable position. It was forced to surrender.

In Dalmatia, by contrast, although the Ottomans initially made significant gains, the Venetians were more successful in the long run. The Turks viewed this part of the war as very much a minor theatre, and thus sent few troops to reinforce their initial success. By the time peace returned in 1669, Venice had made significant territorial gains.

In 1684, in the wake of the Ottoman defeat outside Vienna, the Venetians saw an opportunity to expand at the expense of the Turks and declared war. Financial aid was obtained from the Knights Hospitaller and Savoy and, with this, large numbers of German mercenaries were hired. The main offensive was in the Morea (Peloponnese), and by 1687 this was nearly wholly in Venetian hands. The last Ottoman holdout was taken in 1690. With the Morea taken, the Venetians then moved onto central Greece, arriving at Athens in September of that year. The resulting siege of the Ottoman garrison on the Acropolis lasted only six days and is mainly notable for the destruction caused when a Venetian shell hit the Parthenon, which was being used by the Turks as a magazine. Despite this success, the Venetians withdrew from central Greece, as their positions were too exposed. In 1692 an Ottoman counter-offensive into the Morea met with some success, but was, in the end, a failure, and the Venetians remained in possession. This was confirmed by the peace treaty concluded at the start of 1699. A Venetian attempt in 1692 to recapture Crete was a failure.

TROOP NOTES

The Venetians relied heavily on mercenary infantry, especially from Germany, where a number of states hired out whole regiments to the Venetians for service. These states included Bayreuth, Waldeck, Wolfenbuttel, Hessen-Kassel and Hanover. With the start of the War of the League of Augsburg, these contingents dried up as their masters instead hired them out to the Maritime Powers and their allies in the war against France. Despite this, German mercenaries remained common, although they were now recruited by private military entrepreneurs for the Venetians, rather than being sent by princes. Their numbers were usually of the order of 7,000 men in an overall military establishment that never went much above 20,000.

The regular infantry could be supplemented by local troops, often of dubious worth, and local bandit types, more interested in the possibility of loot than in actually fighting for Venice. However, troops from Dalmatia and the Balkans, armed with muskets and the schiavona sword, proved to be useful.

The Venetians were assisted, from time to time, by contingents of troops supplied from the fleet of the Knights Hospitaller. These were mainly equipped with firearms, but they were led by brother knights and similar, who were equipped for hand to hand fighting. We represent this by giving these battle groups Swordsmen melee capability, and recommend that a number of armoured knights are depicted on the musketeer bases.

Stradiots were still used, but now relied on firearms.

LATER VENETIAN COLONIAL STARTER ARMY (FROM 1689)

Commander-in-Chief	1	Field Commander
Sub-Commanders	2	2 x Troop Commander
Mercenary horse	1 BG	4 bases of Mercenary horse; Average, Unarmoured Determined Horse – Impact Pistol, Melee Pistol
Stradiots	1 BG	4 bases of Stradiots: Average, Unarmoured Cavalry – Carbine, Melee Pistol
Stradiots	2 BGs	Each comprising 4 bases of Stradiots: Average, Unarmoured Light Horse – Carbine, Melee Pistol
Venetian and mercenary infantry or militia	3 BGs	Each comprising 6 bases of Venetian and mercenary infantry or militia: 5 bases of Average, Unarmoured Medium Foot – Musket, Bayonet; and 1 base of Average, Unarmoured Heavy Foot – Pike
Dalmatians, Slavs and similar schiavoni	2 BGs	Each comprising 6 bases of Dalmatians, Slavs and similar schiavoni: Average, Unarmoured Medium Foot – Musket, Swordsmen
Bandits, Morlacchi, Maniotes and similar	2 BGs	Each comprising 6 bases of Bandits, Morlacchi, Maniotes and similar: Poor, Unarmoured Warriors – Musket*
Artillery	1 BG	2 bases of Artillery – Average Medium Artillery
Camp	1	Unfortified camp
Total	12 BGs	Camp, 16 mounted bases, 44 foot bases, 3 commanders

BUILDING A CUSTOMISED LIST USING OUR ARMY POINTS

Choose an army based on the maxima and minima in the list below. The following special instructions apply to this army:

- Commanders should be depicted as mercenary horse.

LATER VENETIAN COLONIAL

Territory Types: Agricultural

C-in-C	Great Commander/Field Commander/Troop Commander						80/50/35		1
Sub-commanders	Field Commander						50		0–2
	Troop Commander						35		0–3
Troop name		**Troop Type**			**Capabilities**			**Points per base**	**Bases per BG**	**Total bases**
		Type	Armour	Quality	Shooting	Impact	Melee			
Core Troops										
Mercenary horse	Only before 1650	Horse	Unarmoured	Average	Carbine	–	Pistol	9	4	0–8
				Poor				7		
		Horse	Unarmoured	Average	–	Pistol	Pistol	8	4	
				Poor				6		
	Any date	Determined Horse	Unarmoured	Average	–	Pistol	Pistol	12	4	
				Poor				9		
Stradiots		Light Horse	Unarmoured	Average	Carbine	–	Pistol	9	4	4–12
		Cavalry	Unarmoured	Average	Carbine	–	Pistol	10	4	
Venetian and mercenary infantry or militia	Only before 1689	Medium Foot	Unarmoured	Average	Musket	–	–	8	4	6
		Heavy Foot	Unarmoured	Average	–	Pike	Pike	5	2	
		Medium Foot	Unarmoured	Poor	Musket	–	–	6	4	6
		Heavy Foot	Unarmoured	Poor	–	Pike	Pike	3	2	18–72
	Only from 1689	Medium Foot	Unarmoured	Average	Musket	Bayonet	Bayonet	8	5	6
		Heavy Foot	Unarmoured	Average	–	Pike	Pike	5	1	
		Medium Foot	Unarmoured	Poor	Musket	Bayonet	Bayonet	6	5	6
		Heavy Foot	Unarmoured	Poor	–	Pike	Pike	3	1	

Artillery	Heavy Artillery	–	Average	Heavy Artillery	–	–	25	2	0–2
	Medium Artillery	–	Average	Medium Artillery	–	–	20	2, 3 or 4	0–4
Optional Troops									
Dalmatians, Slavs and similar schiavoni	Medium Foot	Unarmoured	Average	Musket	–	Swordsmen	8	6–8	0–18
Bandits, Morlacchi, Maniotes and similar	Warriors	Unarmoured	Poor	Musket*	–	–	4	6–8	0–18
Maltese marines led by Knights Hospitaller	Medium Foot	Unarmoured	Average	Musket	–	Swordsmen	8	6–8	0–12
Fortifications	Field Fortifications	–	–	–	–	–	3	–	0–18
Fortified camp							24		0–1
Allies									
French allies (Only from 1660 to 1669) – Later Louis XIV French									

(The 0–2 and 0–4 artillery rows share a combined total of 0–4.)

LATER SWEDISH

*T*his list covers Swedish armies from the Treaty of Westphalia in 1648 until 1698. Sweden emerged from the Thirty Years' War as one of the great European powers, despite holding relatively little land in Europe proper, as well as a major power in the Baltic. As its German territories were part of the Holy Roman Empire, it had votes in the Imperial Diet and, along with France, was a guarantor of the Peace of Westphalia. Its powerful army, seen as possibly the best in Europe, was also an invaluable asset in maintaining its influence.

Despite this, Sweden's internal political situation was far from stable, as the militaristic state was now ruled by Gustavus Adolphus' daughter Christina, who steadfastly refused to marry and, to add extra complication, had secretly converted to Catholicism. Christina solved this in 1654 by abdicating in favour of her cousin Karl Gustav, the commander-in-chief of the Swedish armies in the latter stages of the Thirty Years' War, who ascended the throne as Karl X. A soldier of ability, he soon decided that it was in

Sweden's interest to invade the Polish-Lithuanian Commonwealth. One factor in this decision may have been that the high cost of maintaining Sweden's army, which included many mercenaries, was best solved by transferring that cost to another country, where the soldiers could be maintained by the resources and "contributions" of the occupied, rather than being a burden to the Swedes. The Commonwealth, currently in crisis from an internal rebellion and Russian invasion, was the perfect target.

The Swedish invasion was a complete success, with minimal resistance being met. By the end of 1655 they had over-run a large part of the country, and the Polish king, John Casimir, was in exile. However, the Swedish forces were far too small to properly occupy the territory they had won. The Polish nobles sank their differences to fight the invader, and John Casimir returned to Poland. Despite an alliance with Brandenburg-Prussia, who had territorial ambitions of its own in Poland, Karl's position turned for the worse as Russia now intervened to attack the Swedes. However, they

could not maintain the strain of keeping large forces in the field, and a year or so later that pressure eased.

With the situation in Poland worsening, despite a great victory over the Poles at Warsaw in 1656, Karl was presented with an opportunity to leave Poland when Denmark entered the war in 1657. Karl's campaign in Denmark in the winter of 1657/8 is one of the most audacious in military history. Taking advantage of a harsh winter that froze the Great and Little Belts that separated the Danish islands from the mainland, Karl successfully led his now rather small army across the ice. Overawed by this feat, and with Copenhagen under threat, the Danes sued for peace, yielding significant territories to Sweden. Within a few months, however, Karl attacked again without warning and laid siege to Copenhagen. The Danes held out long enough for a Dutch fleet to arrive and relieve the siege by defeating the Swedish navy at Battle of the Sound on 29 October 1658. Negotiations for peace were again opened, Karl dying in 1660 before they were complete, his death giving Sweden the opportunity to make a genuine peace and bring the war to a close.

Karl was succeeded by his son, as Karl XI. As he was only five at the time, however, it was some time before Sweden again found itself involved in a major war. Once again this was a war mainly with the old Baltic rival, Denmark, and is known as the Scanian War from the province invaded by the Danes in 1676. However, the war really started in 1674 when, under pressure from France, who threatened to withhold subsidies Sweden relied on, Sweden invaded Brandenburg to relieve pressure on France, which was engaged in a war with the Dutch and her allies. It appears that Sweden's heart was not really in the war. Her army advanced tentatively from Pomerania, and was defeated in 1675 at Fehrbellin by the Elector of Brandenburg, who had brought his army back from the Rhine to defend his lands. This was a heavy blow to the Swedish aura of military invincibility. Sensing Swedish weakness, the Danes now entered the war, hoping to regain lost territory, whilst Brandenburg seized other lands from them. The entry of Denmark into the war appears to have been the spur the Swedes needed, and they fought back with some elan, the young King himself joining the army. The key battle was the bloody battle of Lund in 1676, where the Swedish army of perhaps 7,500 men defeated a Danish army that was about 50 percent stronger. Casualties were appalling, with around half of each army left dead on the field. This did not end the war, however, and over the next few years the Danes were able to offset Swedish land superiority with naval victories. Eventually, in 1679, a peace was agreed, brokered by France, returning to Sweden all the territory it had lost during the war.

TROOP NOTES

At the start of this period Swedish and Finnish horse were, in theory, armoured with a buffcoat, helmet and breastplate. However, there is evidence that at times they left their helmets, breastplates, and sometimes buffcoats behind and fought unarmoured. Additionally, when the usual source of armour, the Dutch, were opposed to Swedish actions, the supply of equipment would have dried up. We therefore allow the horse to be Armoured or Unarmoured. With the accession of Karl XII in 1697, the horse finally abandoned armour altogether.

From 1676, in the Battle of Halmstad, Swedish horse under Nils Bielke started to fight "in the French manner", attacking sword in hand rather than first using firearms at short range in the manner of the cavalry of Gustavus Adolphus. It is unclear, however, whether this tactic completely replaced the older style, as some units may still have been charging with pistol in hand as late as 1706. We therefore allow Swedish and Finnish horse to be classified as either Impact Mounted or Pistol for the impact phase after 1676.

Similarly, the infantry returned to more aggressive tactics in the Gustavan manner, emphasising a short range volley followed by a charge to contact by musketeers and pikemen. These tactics became known as "*ga pa*", meaning "go on". The first account of this relates to guard battalions at the Battle of Lund in 1676, and it is possible that it was only practiced by such veteran formations to begin with. At this battle they are described as being formed 3 ranks deep, probably

due to the brigades being severely under-strength. At 80 paces from the enemy, the brigade halted and commenced fire by rank. Each rank fired only once and reloaded. When the last rank had reloaded, the brigade resumed the advance to a range of 10–12 paces, where all 3 ranks fired together in a single salvo before charging alongside the pikemen. By the 1690s, however, it appears that ga pa tactics were normal amongst all the front line units, although they now formed up 4 deep and always fired by salvo and not by ranks – 2 ranks at 40 paces and the other 2 at 10 paces or less. With the emphasis on aggression, and the potentially large numbers of horsemen that their enemies could field, the pike remained an important weapon for the Swedish infantry.

LATER SWEDISH STARTER ARMY (1676–1679)		
Commander-in-Chief	1	Field Commander
Sub-Commanders	2	2 x Troop Commander
Swedish or Finnish horse	1 BG	4 bases of Swedish or Finnish horse: Superior, Armoured Determined Horse – Impact Mounted, Swordsmen
Swedish or Finnish horse	1 BG	4 bases of Swedish or Finnish horse: Average, Armoured Determined Horse – Impact Mounted, Swordsmen
Swedish or Finnish horse	1 BG	4 bases of Swedish or Finnish horse: Average, Unarmoured Determined Horse – Impact Pistol, Melee Pistol
Swedish or Finnish infantry battalions	1 BG	6 bases of Swedish or Finnish infantry battalions: 4 bases of Superior, Unarmoured Medium Foot – Salvo, Bayonet; and 2 bases of Superior, Unarmoured Heavy Foot – Pike; and Superior Regimental Guns
Swedish or Finnish infantry battalions	1 BG	6 bases of Swedish or Finnish infantry battalions: 4 bases of Average, Unarmoured Medium Foot – Musket; 2 bases of Average, Unarmoured Heavy Foot – Pike; and Average Regimental Guns
Swedish or Finnish infantry battalions	2 BGs	Each comprising 6 bases of Swedish or Finnish infantry battalions: 4 bases of Average, Unarmoured Medium Foot – Musket; and 2 bases of Average, Unarmoured Heavy Foot – Pike
Dragoons	1 BG	3 bases of Dragoons: Average, Unarmoured Dragoons – Musket
Field artillery	1 BG	2 bases of Field artillery – Average Medium Artillery
Camp	1	Unfortified camp
Total	9 BGs	Camp, 12 mounted bases, 29 foot bases, 3 commanders

BUILDING A CUSTOMISED LIST USING OUR ARMY POINTS

Choose an army based on the maxima and minima in the list below. The following special instructions apply to this army:

- Commanders should be depicted as Swedish and Finnish horse.
- As usual, Regimental Guns must be the same quality as the battle group.

LATER SWEDISH

Territory Types: Agricultural, Woodlands, Hilly

C-in-C	Great Commander/Field Commander/Troop Commander			80/50/35	1	
Sub-commanders	Field Commander			50	0–2	
	Troop Commander			35	0–3	

Troop name		Troop Type			Capabilities			Points per base	Bases per BG	Total bases
		Type	Armour	Quality	Shooting	Impact	Melee			
Core Troops										
Swedish or Finnish horse	Only before 1697	Determined Horse	Armoured	Superior	–	Pistol	Pistol	21	4	8–40
				Average				15		
	Only from 1676 to 1696	Determined Horse	Armoured	Superior	–	Impact Mounted	Swordsmen	23	4	
				Average				17		
	Only from 1676	Determined Horse	Unarmoured	Superior	–	Impact Mounted	Swordsmen	20	4	
				Average				14		
	Any date	Determined Horse	Unarmoured	Superior	–	Pistol	Pistol	18	4	
				Average				12		
Swedish or Finnish infantry battalions	Only before 1676	Medium Foot	Unarmoured	Superior	Musket	–	–	11	4	6	0–24	12–60
		Heavy Foot	Unarmoured	Superior	–	Pike	Pike	8	2	
	Only from 1676	Medium Foot	Unarmoured	Superior	Salvo	Salvo	–	11	4	6	0–24
		Heavy Foot	Unarmoured	Superior	–	Pike	Pike	8	2	
	Only from 1696	Medium Foot	Unarmoured	Superior	Salvo	Salvo + Bayonet	Bayonet	11	4	6	0–24
		Heavy Foot	Unarmoured	Superior	–	Pike	Pike	8	2	
	Only before 1680	Medium Foot	Unarmoured	Average	Musket	–	–	8	4	6	12–60
		Heavy Foot	Unarmoured	Average	–	Pike	Pike	5	2	
	Only from 1680	Medium Foot	Unarmoured	Average	Salvo	Salvo	–	8	4	6	12–60
		Heavy Foot	Unarmoured	Average	–	Pike	Pike	5	2	
	Only from 1696	Medium Foot	Unarmoured	Average	Salvo	Salvo + Bayonet	Bayonet	8	4	6	
		Heavy Foot	Unarmoured	Average	–	Pike	Pike	5	2	
	Any date	Medium Foot	Unarmoured	Poor	Musket	–	–	6	4	6	0–24
		Heavy Foot	Unarmoured	Poor	–	Pike	Pike	3	2	
Battalion guns		Regimental Guns	–	Superior	Regimental Guns	Regimental Guns	–	12	n/a	0–1 per non–Poor infantry battalions BG
				Average				9		
Light artillery		Light Artillery	–	Average	Light Artillery	–	–	12	2	2–4
Field artillery		Medium Artillery	–	Average	Medium Artillery	–	–	20	2, 3 or 4	
Optional Troops										
Dragoons		Dragoons	Unarmoured	Average	Musket	–	–	8	3 or 4	0–8
Allies										

Brandenburg-Prussian allies (Only before 1658) – Later German States

LATER DUTCH

This list covers the armies of the United Provinces from the end of the Thirty Years' War in 1648 until William of Orange became King of England in 1688, after which their armies operated together.

The Dutch Republic emerged from the Thirty Years' War recognised by Spain as a state in its own right as part of the Peace of Münster, and the wider Peace of Westphalia which ended the war. This also confirmed that the Republic was no longer part of the Holy Roman Empire.

With its natural enemy, Spain, utterly bankrupt as a result of its participation in the Thirty Years' War, and its continuing war with France until the Peace of the Pyrenees in 1659, the Republic was not faced with a land war in Europe until the French invaded in 1672. There were, however, three naval wars fought against England in 1652–54, 1665–67 and 1672–74, the last overlapping with the Franco-Dutch war of 1672–78. Overall, the Dutch were successful in these three wars, their achievements including the burning of a number of English ships in the apparently safe anchorage of the Medway, and knocking England out of the Franco-Dutch war in 1674.

The Franco-Dutch war, starting in 1672, was a much more serious affair, and threatened the very existence of the Republic. Louis XIV had been angered, and no doubt disappointed, by the reaction of the Dutch to his attempt to take over the Spanish Netherlands in the War of Devolution. Previously the Dutch had been allies of the French against the Spanish, but Louis appears to have failed to anticipate that the Republic would prefer a weak Spain as a neighbour to a strong and aggressive France. The Dutch were unprepared to meet the French onslaught, the army having been somewhat neglected in favour of the navy, so the French were able to rapidly over-run large parts of the country. The resulting political unrest led to the lynching of Johan de Witt, who had led the Republic successfully through the first two Anglo-Dutch wars, and the appointment of William of Orange to the position of Stadtholder and commander of the Dutch army. With no real means to stop the French, the Dutch were forced to flood the countryside to prevent the French advancing on their main cities.

The time gained by the flooding allowed the Dutch to strengthen their army and build an alliance against the French. This included Brandenburg-Prussia, Austria and Spain. The allies now counter-attacked, although, as was typical of the time, this was a cautious war of manoeuvre and siege rather than of pitched battles. This attritional style of warfare probably suited the allies more than France, who generally got the better of what battles there were, but were less well-placed for a long war. The war ended in 1678 with the Dutch back in possession of all they had started with, as Louis was satisfied with gains from the Spanish in Flanders.

Dutch Guards Officer

Dutch Guards Infantry

TROOP NOTES

Dutch cavalry was considered poor by nearly all of their contemporaries, often being defeated by French cavalry forces far fewer in number. However, as the French cavalry were, at the time, the best in Europe by a long way, we do not consider this enough evidence to justify making all the Dutch cavalry Poor quality.

Dutch infantry appear to have retained armour for the pikemen at least at the start of this period, and the guards may have done so throughout.

LATER DUTCH STARTER ARMY (BEFORE 1680)		
Commander-in-Chief	1	Field Commander
Sub-Commanders	2	2 x Troop Commander
Dutch cavalry	2 BGs	Each comprising 4 bases of Dutch cavalry: Average, Unarmoured Determined Horse – Impact Pistol, Melee Pistol
Dutch cavalry	2 BGs	Each comprising 4 bases of Dutch cavalry: Poor, Unarmoured Determined Horse – Impact Pistol, Melee Pistol
Dutch guard infantry	1 BG	6 bases of Dutch guard infantry: 4 bases of Superior, Unarmoured Medium Foot – Musket; 2 bases of Superior, Armoured Heavy Foot – Pike; and Superior Regimental Guns
Dutch, Walloon, Swiss and other line infantry	3 BGs	Each comprising 6 bases of Dutch, Walloon, Swiss and other line infantry: 4 bases of Average, Unarmoured Medium Foot – Musket; 2 bases of Average, Armoured Heavy Foot – Pike; and Average Regimental Guns
Dutch dragoons	1 BG	4 bases of Dutch dragoons: Average, Unarmoured Dragoons – Musket
Artillery	1 BG	2 bases of Artillery – Average Medium Artillery
Camp	1	Unfortified camp
Total	10 BGs	Camp, 16 mounted bases, 30 foot bases, 3 commanders

BUILDING A CUSTOMISED LIST USING OUR ARMY POINTS

Choose an army based on the maxima and minima in the list below. The following special instructions apply to this army:

+ Commanders should be depicted as Dutch cavalry.

+ At least half the battle groups of Dutch cavalry fielded must be Poor quality.

+ As usual, Regimental Guns must be the same quality as the battle group.

Brandenburg Regiment Infantryman

LATER DUTCH

LATER DUTCH									
Territory Types: Agricultural									
C-in-C	Great Commander/Field Commander/Troop Commander						80/50/35		1
Sub-commanders	Field Commander						50		0–2
	Troop Commander						35		0–3
Troop name	**Troop Type**			**Capabilities**			**Points per base**	**Bases per BG**	**Total bases**
	Type	Armour	Quality	Shooting	Impact	Melee			
Core Troops									
Dutch cavalry	Determined Horse	Unarmoured	Average	–	Pistol	Pistol	12	4	4–20
			Poor				9		
Dutch guard infantry	Only before 1680	Medium Foot	Unarmoured	Superior	Musket	–	–	11	4	6	0–12
		Heavy Foot	Armoured	Superior	–	Pike	Pike	9	2	
	Only from 1680	Medium Foot	Unarmoured	Superior	Musket	Bayonet	Bayonet	11	4	6
		Heavy Foot	Armoured	Superior	–	Pike	Pike	9	2	
		Medium Foot	Unarmoured	Superior	Musket	Bayonet	Bayonet	11	4	6
		Heavy Foot	Unarmoured	Superior	–	Pike	Pike	8	2	
Dutch, Walloon, Swiss and other line infantry	Only before 1680	Medium Foot	Unarmoured	Average	Musket	–	–	8	4	6	12–72
		Heavy Foot	Armoured	Average	–	Pike	Pike	6	2	
	Only from 1680	Medium Foot	Unarmoured	Average	Musket	Bayonet	Bayonet	8	4	6
		Heavy Foot	Unarmoured	Average	–	Pike	Pike	5	2	
3-pdr battalion guns	Regimental Guns	–	Superior	Regimental Guns	Regimental Guns	–	12	n/a	0–1 per guard or line infantry BG
			Average				9		
Dutch dragoons	Dragoons	Unarmoured	Average	Musket	–	–	8	3–4	3–6
Artillery	Heavy Artillery	–	Average	Heavy Artillery	–	–	25	2, 3 or 4	2–4
	Medium Artillery	–	Average	Medium Artillery	–	–	20	2, 3 or 4	
Optional Troops									
Dutch garrison infantry	Only before 1680	Medium Foot	Unarmoured	Poor	Musket	–	–	6	4	6	0–24
		Heavy Foot	Unarmoured	Poor	–	Pike	Pike	3	2	
	Only from 1680	Medium Foot	Unarmoured	Poor	Musket	Bayonet	Bayonet	6	4	6
		Heavy Foot	Unarmoured	Poor	–	Pike	Pike	3	2	
Allies									
Austrian allies (Only from 1673 to 1678) – Habsburg Austrian Imperial									
Brandenburg-Prussian allies (Only from 1674 to 1678) – Later German States									
Hanoverian and Osnabrück allies (Only in 1668) – Later German States									
Spanish allies (Only from 1672) – Later Spanish (Flanders options)									

LATER DUTCH ALLIES

Allied commander			Field Commander/Troop Commander			40/25		1
Troop name		**Troop Type**			**Capabilities**		**Points per base**	**Bases per BG**	**Total bases**
		Type	Armour	Quality	Shooting	Impact	Melee			

Troop name		Type	Armour	Quality	Shooting	Impact	Melee	**Points per base**	**Bases per BG**	**Total bases**
Dutch cavalry		Determined Horse	Unarmoured	Average	–	Pistol	Pistol	12	4	4–8
				Poor				9		
Dutch guard infantry	Only before 1680	Medium Foot	Unarmoured	Superior	Musket	–	–	11	4	6	0–6
		Heavy Foot	Armoured	Superior	–	Pike	Pike	9	2		
	Only from 1680	Medium Foot	Unarmoured	Superior	Musket	Bayonet	Bayonet	11	4	6	
		Heavy Foot	Armoured	Superior	–	Pike	Pike	9	2		
		Medium Foot	Unarmoured	Superior	Musket	Bayonet	Bayonet	11	4	6	
		Heavy Foot	Unarmoured	Superior	–	Pike	Pike	8	2		
Dutch, Walloon, Swiss and other line infantry	Only before 1680	Medium Foot	Unarmoured	Average	Musket	–	–	8	4	6	6–30
		Heavy Foot	Armoured	Average	–	Pike	Pike	6	2		
	Only from 1680	Medium Foot	Unarmoured	Average	Musket	Bayonet	Bayonet	8	4	6	
		Heavy Foot	Unarmoured	Average	–	Pike	Pike	5	2		
3-pdr battalion guns		Regimental Guns	–	Superior	Regimental Guns	Regimental Guns	–	12	n/a	0–1 per guard or line infantry BG
				Average				9		
Dutch dragoons		Dragoons	Unarmoured	Average	Musket	–	–	8	2	0–2
Artillery		Heavy Artillery	–	Average	Heavy Artillery	–	–	25	2	0–2
		Medium Artillery	–	Average	Medium Artillery	–	–	20	2	

LATER DANISH

*F*or the Danes, the Thirty Years' War had been a disaster, with a series of defeats resulting in Denmark under Christian IV losing its Baltic supremacy to Sweden. Christian died in 1648 and was succeeded by his son as Frederick III, after he agreed to restrictions on royal powers.

In 1657, seeing Sweden bogged down in a war in Poland, Frederick saw the opportunity for Denmark to regain some of its lost ground, and so embarked on war. Unfortunately, the decision to go to war backfired on Frederick somewhat spectacularly. The Swedish king, Karl X, audaciously attacked

Denmark in the severe winter of 1657/8, crossing the frozen straights between the mainland and Danish islands to arrive outside Copenhagen. Denmark was forced to sue for peace and give up significant territories. Peace, however, was short-lived, and within months the Swedes had recommenced hostilities, with the aim of capturing Copenhagen and thus, possibly, conquering Denmark in its entirety. However, the Danes resisted and a major Swedish assault was beaten off with heavy losses. The Swedes were forced to withdraw when the Dutch sent a fleet to assist the

Danes, the Dutch defeating the Swedish navy while the Danes, unable to intervene because of adverse winds, looked on. Following the death of Karl X a real peace was signed, but this confirmed many of the territorial losses suffered by Denmark.

Despite this setback, Frederick benefitted greatly from the war as he used the popularity he had gained by resisting Sweden to institute one of the most comprehensive absolutist regimes in Europe, with the crown having almost unlimited powers.

Frederick's son Christian V was also, inevitably, involved in a war with Sweden, known as the Scanian War after the name of the lands (Scania) that the Danes attempted to regain from Sweden, having been forced to cede them at the end of the previous conflict. The war started in 1675 with Denmark invading Scania. They were undoubtedly encouraged by the defeat of the Swedes by Brandenburg-Prussia at the Battle of Fehrbellin the previous year. Although the Danish offensive was initially a great success, Swedish counter-offensives recaptured much of the Danish gains. In the end this was a war with no definite victor, with the Swedish navy defeated in a number of engagements and the Danish army defeated in Scania by the Swedes, who themselves were defeated by Brandenburg-Prussia in Sweden's German possessions. The war ended in 1679 when the allies of the major combatants themselves came to terms, and brought pressure on their allies to do likewise. Unfortunately for Denmark, the strongest power, France, was allied to Sweden, and thus the peace was somewhat unfavourable.

Fynske Regiment Infantryman

This list covers Danish armies from 1649 to 1698. It should be noted that at this time Norway was part of the Danish kingdom, but had a separate, smaller, military establishment, although this was organised along the same lines as the Danes'.

TROOP NOTES

As late as 1676, infantry companies were to comprise 24 pikemen and 60 musketeers. We represent these proportions by battle groups of bases of pikemen and 4 of musketeers. By the 1670s bayonets were in use. In 1678, by royal decree, pikes were to be abandoned and the musketeers were to be equipped with *svinfjer* (swinefeathers) as protection against enemy mounted. As this was during the Scanian War, it is possible that it was not universally followed until the post war period, so we allow battle groups both with pikes and without for a short period.

Each infantry battalion could have 2 small 3-pdr guns attached throughout this period.

Before 1675 there was only a small lifeguard of horse. After this a full regiment was raised, although it was not always at full strength.

Mercenary regiments of Germans, both horse and foot, were raised in times of need. Despite their origins, they appear to have been equipped and fought in the same manner as native Danish and Norwegian troops.

In 1677 and 1678 a small number of Austrian auxiliaries were attached to the Danish army. These were kürassiere, dragoons and a very small number of Croats. Unfortunately the latter were too few, 80 at the most, to be represented in the army list, but players may like to include the odd Croat figure on the Austrian kürassiere bases for colour.

LATER DANISH STARTER ARMY (FROM 1678)		
Commander-in-Chief	1	Field Commander
Sub-Commanders	2	2 x Troop Commander
Horse guards	1 BG	2 bases of Horse guards: Superior, Unarmoured Determined Horse – Impact Pistol, Melee Pistol
Danish horse	3 BGs	Each comprising 4 bases of Danish horse: Average, Unarmoured Determined Horse – Impact Pistol, Melee Pistol
Danish, Norwegian and German infantry	4 BGs	Each comprising 6 bases of Danish, Norwegian and German infantry: Average, Unarmoured Medium Foot – Musket, Bayonet
Dragoons	1 BG	3 bases of Dragoons: Average, Unarmoured Dragoons – Musket
Field artillery	1 BG	2 bases of Field artillery – Average Medium Artillery
Svinfjer	6 Svinfjer	– Portable obstacles to cover 3 files each of two Danish, Norwegian and German infantry battle groups
Camp	1	Unfortified camp
Total	10 BGs	Camp, 14 mounted bases, 29 foot bases, 3 commanders

BUILDING A CUSTOMISED LIST USING OUR ARMY POINTS

Choose an army based on the maxima and minima in the list below. The following special instructions apply to this army:

• Commanders should be depicted as Danish horse or horse guards.

• Only one battle group of Horse guards can be fielded.

• As usual, Regimental Guns must be the same quality as the battle group.

LATER DANISH										
Territory Types: Agricultural										
C-in-C	Great Commander/Field Commander/Troop Commander						80/50/35		1	
Sub-commanders	Field Commander						50		0–2	
	Troop Commander						35		0–3	
Troop name	Troop Type			Capabilities			Points per base	Bases per BG	Total bases	
	Type	Armour	Quality	Shooting	Impact	Melee				
Core Troops										
Danish horse	Determined Horse	Unarmoured	Average	–	Pistol	Pistol	12	4	4–24	
Foot guards	Only before 1670	Medium Foot	Unarmoured	Superior	Musket	–	–	11	4	6	0–12
		Heavy Foot	Unarmoured	Superior	–	Pike	Pike	8	2	
	Only from 1670 to 1680	Medium Foot	Unarmoured	Superior	Musket	Bayonet	Bayonet	11	4	6
		Heavy Foot	Unarmoured	Superior	–	Pike	Pike	8	2	
	Only from 1678	Medium Foot	Unarmoured	Superior	Musket	Bayonet	Bayonet	12	6	
Danish, Norwegian and German infantry	Only before 1670	Medium Foot	Unarmoured	Average	Musket	–	–	8	4	6	12–72
		Heavy Foot	Unarmoured	Average	–	Pike	Pike	5	2	
	Only from 1670 to 1680	Medium Foot	Unarmoured	Average	Musket	Bayonet	Bayonet	8	4	6
		Heavy Foot	Unarmoured	Average	–	Pike	Pike	5	2	
	Only from 1678	Medium Foot	Unarmoured	Average	Musket	Bayonet	Bayonet	9	6	
3-pdr battalion guns	Regimental Guns	–	Superior	Regimental Guns	Regimental Guns	–	12	n/a	0–1 per foot guards or Danish, Norwegian and German infantry BG
			Average				9		

Troop name		Type	Armour	Quality				Points	Bases	Per unit	Total
Field artillery		Medium Artillery	–	Average	Medium Artillery	–	–	20	2, 3 or 4	0–4	2–4
		Heavy Artillery	–	Average	Heavy Artillery	–	–	25	2	0–2	
Optional Troops											
Dragoons		Dragoons	Unarmoured	Average	Musket	–	–	8	3–4	0–8	
Horse guards	Only from 1675	Determined Horse	Unarmoured	Superior	–	Pistol	Pistol	18	2–4	0–4	
Svinfjer to cover 3 files of each Foot Guard or Danish, Norwegian and German infantry	Only before 1678	Portable Defences	–	–	–	–	–	3	–	0–12	
	Only from 1678									Any	
Danish and Norwegian garrison infantry	Only before 1670	Medium Foot	Unarmoured	Poor	Musket	–	–	6	4	6	0–24
		Heavy Foot	Unarmoured	Poor	–	Pike	Pike	3	2		
	Only from 1670 to 1680	Medium Foot	Unarmoured	Poor	Musket	Bayonet	Bayonet	6	4	6	
		Heavy Foot	Unarmoured	Poor	–	Pike	Pike	3	2		
	Only from 1678	Medium Foot	Unarmoured	Poor	Musket	Bayonet	Bayonet	7	6		
Austrian kürassiere	Only from 1677 to 1678	Determined Horse	Armoured	Average	Carbine	–	Pistol	16	2	0–2	
		Determined Horse	Armoured	Average	–	Pistol	Pistol	15	2		
Allies											

Brandenburg-Prussian allies (Only from 1675 to 1678) – Later German States

Dutch allies (Only from 1658 to 1659, cannot include mounted troops) – Later Dutch

HABSBURG AUSTRIAN IMPERIAL

This list covers the armies of Habsburg Austria, the *Kaiserliche Armee* as opposed to the *Reichsarmee* of the Holy Roman Empire, from the end of the Thirty Years' War until 1698.

At the end of the Thirty Years' War the hereditary Habsburg lands of Austria were bankrupt and the influence of the Emperor within the Holy Roman Empire was reduced, with two foreign powers, Sweden and France, appointed as guarantors of German liberties – partly to ensure that the Emperor's power was curtailed. However, by the end of the period of this list Austria was once again a major power with a significant say in European politics.

In the immediate aftermath of the Thirty Years' War, for the remainder of the reign of Ferdinand III, Austria went through something of a rebuilding process, disbanding most of the army, re-establishing the economy and the power of the crown, whilst coming to terms with the changed relationship with the Holy Roman Empire and the new European superpower of France. Fortunately, France was still involved with its war with Spain and its internal troubles of the Fronde, and on the eastern front the Turks remained quiet. Ferdinand died in 1658, and was succeeded by his son Leopold, who was to reign for the rest of the period covered by this list, with Austria benefitting from this piece of stability.

War with the Turks resumed in 1663 when a massive Ottoman army invaded Habsburg Hungary – in response to the Austrians sending an army under Montecuccoli into Transylvania to prevent it falling under Ottoman control. Being heavily outnumbered by the Turks, Leopold summoned an Imperial Diet to obtain assistance from the Holy Roman Empire. This was successful, with large contingents being sent by Saxony, Bavaria and Brandenburg, and an additional 6,000 men, somewhat surprisingly, by Louis XIV, under Jean de Coligny-Saligny. With this army Montecuccoli was able to defeat the Ottomans at the Battle of St Gotthard, catching them crossing a river, with the French contingent playing an important part. As a result of this somewhat surprising defeat, the Turks agreed a 20-year truce, which was of great benefit to the Austrians as it meant they could intervene in Western Europe without the risk of a two-front war.

In 1672 Leopold was forced to send troops to the Rhineland to intervene in the Franco-Dutch war to prevent Louis XIV from conquering the Dutch Republic. Once again he sent his great general Montecuccoli who, until his retirement from service in 1675, led the Imperial army with great success in an intricate war of manoeuvre against the great French marshal Turenne. Austrian troops also participated in joint actions with other German states under the banner of the Holy Roman Empire. The war ended in 1678 to the advantage of France, and the Emperor's position in Germany was somewhat weakened, although in general the German states bore the worst of the treaty.

In 1672 rebellion broke out in the Habsburg Hungarian possessions, mainly as a result of Leopold's attempt to impose autocratic Imperial rule on the Hungarians, sweeping away their ancient constitution. This, coupled with Austria's apparent pre-occupation with the actions of Louis XIV in the west, encouraged the Turks to once again prepare for war, this time with the aim of capturing Vienna itself. This led to one of the most famous sieges of the early modern period when, in 1683, a large Turkish army marched into Austria and placed Vienna under siege. Once again the Austrians were unable to field a large enough army to prevent this, and turned to their allies to provide troops to raise the siege, which was being strongly prosecuted in the face of determined resistance from the garrison led by Count Ernst Rüdiger Starhemberg. Once again Saxony and Bavaria, plus other German states, rallied to the Emperor, partly motivated by the desire to defend Christendom, and this time a significant Polish army under their new king Jan Sobieski also arrived to fight the Turks. This combined army marched to Vienna and, on 12 September, defeated the Turks with heavy losses, thus raising the siege.

Sachsen-Koburg Musketeer

With the Turks in retreat, the Austrians, with large German contingents, now counter-attacked into Turkish Hungary, to recapture land that had been under Turkish control since the early 16th century. With this successful advance, the Hungarian rebellion crumbled, most of the rebels realising that they were in no position to resist the victorious Austrian armies. The run of victories, and recapture of land, continued until 1689, when the exploits of Louis XIV once again turned the focus of attention westwards, especially for the German princes on whom the Austrians relied heavily for troops. For a while the war in Hungary took on the aspect of a secondary theatre of war as Austria struggled to come to terms with, and find resources for, a war on two fronts. Exceptionally, she was able to do so. Initially, however, a Turkish counter-attack had to be weathered, and it wasn't until the mid 1690s that Austrian armies could once again resume major offensive activities. The breakthrough really came with the appointment of Prince Eugene of Savoy to command in Hungary. Following his crushing defeat of the Turks at the Battle of Zenta in 1697, the Ottomans were forced to sue for peace, which was finally signed in 1699.

In the meantime, Austrian troops had also been engaged in the west in the War of the League of Augsburg, but mainly as part of the Reichsarmee of the Holy Roman Empire. Additionally, Prince Eugene led an Austrian army into Savoy in support of his cousin, Victor Amadeus II, to prevent the French from conquering Savoy and moving into northern Italy, which would threaten Austria from the south. Whilst the troops on the Rhine engaged in yet another war of manoeuvre and sieges, the Imperial army in Savoy were more active, even invading France in 1692. However, when Savoy came to terms with Louis in 1696, the Imperial troops went home. The Peace of Ryswick in 1697 brought the war to close. Despite the Emperor being opposed to it, all of his allies agreed to the peace and so he was forced to make peace as well.

TROOP NOTES

Austria was one of the first European states to establish a standing army when, in 1649, an Imperial decree established 9 permanent infantry, 9 permanent kürassiere and 1 permanent dragoon regiments, as well as a small artillery train. Despite the fact that all units were part of the Imperial army, the individual regiments were raised by, and considered the property of, their colonels, who were known as *Oberst-Inhaber* or colonel-proprietors. On the death or retirement of the colonel, the regiment was handed over to a new owner, often as a gift from the Emperor.

As with most contemporaries, the Imperial infantry reduced the number of pikes over the course of this period, and after about 1690 they were not always used. Bayonets were not generally used until the War of the Spanish Succession, and for defence against enemy horsemen the infantry tended to rely on "Spanish riders" (an alternative name for Swedish/swine feathers) often combined into a chevaux-de-frise. Whilst this proved effective when fighting the Turks, as Austrian armies were often tactically defensive, it was less useful in Western Europe, where warfare was more fluid.

As well as representing lower quality Imperial regiments, Poor infantry also represent the *Landsregimenter* units raised during the later stages of the war with the Turks. These were quasi-regular home defence regiments, officered by the local nobility. Despite being primarily raised to defend their homelands, they could, on occasion, be used abroad, although this sometimes led them to mutiny, as this was seen as an underhand method of conscripting them into the regular army.

Austrian kürassiere now formed up 3 ranks deep, or even just 2 when not facing the Turks. Against the Turks they appear to have returned to firearms tactics, discharging their carbines and pistols at range before closing. In the west it appears they were less attached to firearms tactics, and more likely to close to contact as a first choice.

The first regular hussar regiment was raised in 1688. Its equipment, although now standardised, was more or less the same as the Crabats, etc. had been using for decades.

From the 1680s until the end of this period, seeing which way the war was going, many Hungarian rebels (or ex-rebels) joined the Imperial armies in fighting the Ottomans. As these remained intrinsically unreliable, we classify them as allies.

Owing to the high cost of maintaining the army, the Habsburg Emperor relied heavily on contingents supplied to him in times of need by various German states. Although these usually came with strings attached, monetary or political or both, they usually operated fairly effectively with the Imperial units. This, coupled with the regular appointment of their leaders to high Imperial command, means that such contingents are not treated as allies.

From 1683 to 1685, Heironim Lubomirski supplied a Polish contingent to fight the Turks and Tatars. This comprised 2 regiments of cuirassiers, identical to the Imperial ones, 1 regiment of dragoons, again identical to the Imperials, and 4 or 6 "banners" of pancerni-style mail-armoured cavalry armed with bows, spears, pistols and sabres. A few carbines were also carried. As the cuirassiers and dragoons were not distinguishable from the Imperial troops, they are not given a separate entry in the list.

HABSBURG AUSTRIAN IMPERIAL STARTER ARMY (EASTERN 1683-1685)		
Commander-in-Chief	1	Field Commander
Sub-Commanders	2	2 x Troop Commander
Imperial kürassiere	1 BG	4 bases of Imperial kürassiere: Average, Armoured Determined Horse – Carbine, Melee Pistol
German cavalry contingents	1 BG	4 bases of German cavalry contingents: Average, Unarmoured Determined Horse – Carbine, Melee Pistol
Lubomirski's Poles	1 BG	4 bases of Lubomirski's Poles: Average, Armoured Cavalry – Bow, Melee Pistol
Crabaten, Ungaren	1 BG	4 bases of Crabaten, Ungaren: Average, Unarmoured Light Horse – Carbine, Melee Pistol
Imperial infantry	1 BG	6 bases of Imperial infantry: 5 bases of Superior, Unarmoured Medium Foot; – Musket; 1 base of Superior, Unarmoured Heavy Foot – Pike; and Superior Regimental Guns
Imperial infantry	1 BG	6 bases of Imperial infantry: 5 bases of Average, Unarmoured Medium Foot – Musket; 1 base of Average, Unarmoured Heavy Foot – Pike; and Average Regimental Guns
Imperial infantry	1 BG	6 bases of Imperial infantry: 5 bases of Average, Unarmoured Medium Foot – Musket; and 1 base of Average, Unarmoured Heavy Foot – Pike
Hungarian, Croatian and other militärgrenze infantry	1 BG	6 bases of Hungarian, Croatian and other militärgrenze infantry: 6 bases of Average, Unarmoured Light Foot – Musket
Dragoner	1 BG	3 bases of Dragoner: Average, Unarmoured Dragoons – Musket
Artillery	1 BG	2 bases of Artillery – Average Medium Artillery
Camp	1	Unfortified camp
Total	10 BGs	Camp, 16 mounted bases, 29 foot bases, 3 commanders

BUILDING A CUSTOMISED LIST USING OUR ARMY POINTS

Choose an army based on the maxima and minima in the list below. The following special instructions apply to this army:

- Commanders should be depicted as Imperial kürassiere or German cavalry.
- As usual, Regimental Guns must be the same quality as the battle group.
- Armies must be designated as either Eastern (i.e. those facing the Turks) or Western.

HABSBURG AUSTRIAN IMPERIAL										
Territory Types: Agricultural, Hilly, Woodland										
C-in-C		Great Commander/Field Commander/Troop Commander						80/50/35		1
Sub-commanders		Field Commander						50		0–2
		Troop Commander						35		0–3
Troop name		Troop Type			Capabilities			Points per base	Bases per BG	Total bases
		Type	Armour	Quality	Shooting	Impact	Melee			
Core Troops										
Imperial kürassiere	Any	Determined Horse	Armoured	Average	Carbine	–	Pistol	16	4	4–24
	Only in Western armies	Determined Horse	Armoured	Average	–	Pistol	Pistol	15	4	
Imperial infantry	Only before 1675	Medium Foot	Unarmoured	Superior	Musket	–	–	11	4	0–12
		Heavy Foot	Unarmoured	Superior	–	Pike	Pike	8	2	
	Only from 1675	Medium Foot	Unarmoured	Superior	Musket	–	–	11	5	0–12
		Heavy Foot	Unarmoured	Superior	–	Pike	Pike	8	1	
	Only from 1691	Medium Foot	Unarmoured	Superior	Musket	–	–	10	6	
	Only before 1675	Medium Foot	Unarmoured	Average	Musket	–	–	8	4	18–48
		Heavy Foot	Unarmoured	Average	–	Pike	Pike	5	2	
		Medium Foot	Unarmoured	Poor	Musket	–	–	6	4	
		Heavy Foot	Unarmoured	Poor	–	Pike	Pike	3	2	
	Only from 1675	Medium Foot	Unarmoured	Average	Musket	–	–	8	5	12–48
		Heavy Foot	Unarmoured	Average	–	Pike	Pike	5	1	
		Medium Foot	Unarmoured	Poor	Musket	–	–	6	5	
		Heavy Foot	Unarmoured	Poor	–	Pike	Pike	3	1	
	Only from 1691	Medium Foot	Unarmoured	Average	Musket	–	–	7	6	
				Poor				5		
3-pdr regimental guns	Regimental Guns	–	Superior	Regimental Guns	Regimental Guns	–	12	n/a	0–1 per Imperial infantry BG
			Average				9		
			Poor				7		
Artillery	Heavy Artillery	–	Average	Heavy Artillery	–	–	25	2	0–2
	Medium Artillery	–	Average	Medium Artillery	–	–	20	2, 3 or 4	2–4
	Light Artillery	–	Average	Light Artillery	–	–	12	2, 3 or 4	0–2

Optional Troops										
Crabaten, Ungaren and, from 1688, regular hussars		Light Horse	Unarmoured	Average	Carbine	–	Pistol	9	4	0–12
Dragoner		Dragoons	Unarmoured	Average	Musket	–	–	8	3 or 4	0–8
German infantry contingents	Only before 1689	Medium Foot	Unarmoured	Average	Musket	–	–	8	4	0–48
		Heavy Foot	Unarmoured	Average	–	Pike	Pike	5	2 (6)	
		Medium Foot	Unarmoured	Poor	Musket	–	–	6	4	
		Heavy Foot	Unarmoured	Poor	–	Pike	Pike	3	2 (6)	
	Only from 1689	Medium Foot	Unarmoured	Average	Musket	Bayonet	Bayonet	9	6	0–48 in Western armies, 0–16 in Eastern armies
				Poor				7		
German cavalry contingents	Only before 1689	Determined Horse	Armoured	Average	–	Pistol	Pistol	15	4	0–16 in Eastern armies before 1689 or Western armies, 0–8 in Eastern armies from 1689
				Poor				11		
		Determined Horse	Armoured	Average	Carbine	–	Pistol	16	4	
				Poor				12		
	Any date	Determined Horse	Unarmoured	Average	–	Pistol	Pistol	12	4	
				Poor				9		
		Determined Horse	Unarmoured	Average	Carbine	–	Pistol	13	4	
				Poor				10		
Lubomirski's Poles	Only Eastern armies from 1683 to 1685	Cavalry	Armoured	Average	Bow	–	Pistol	12	4–6	0–6
Hungarian, Croatian and other militärgrenze infantry	Only Eastern armies	Medium Foot	Unarmoured	Average	Musket	–	Swords men	8	6–8	0–12
		Light Foot	Unarmoured	Average	Musket	–	–	7	6–8	
"Spanish riders" or chevaux-de-frise to cover 3 files of each Imperial infantry BG	Only from 1675	Portable Defences	–	–	–	–	–	3	–	Any
Fortifications		Field Fortifications	–	–	–	–	–	3	–	0–18
Fortified camp								24		0–1

Allies
French allies (Only Eastern armies from 1663 to 1664) – Later Louis XIV French
Hungarian rebel allies (Only Eastern armies from 1680) – Hungarian Kuruc Rebellion

Special Campaigns

Relief of Vienna and aftermath, 1683

Up to ⅓ of the army's points can be spent on troops from the Later Polish and Lithuanian list and up to ⅓ on troops from the Later German States army list. Minima, other than commanders, must be adhered to, but otherwise any eligible troops may be selected. No allies are allowed. All commanders count in line of command to all troops in the army. The C-in-C is Polish.

HABSBURG AUSTRIAN IMPERIAL ALLIES

Allied commander		Field Commander/Troop Commander					40/25	1	
Troop name		**Troop Type**			**Capabilities**		**Points per base**	**Bases per BG**	**Total bases**
		Type	Armour	Quality	Shooting	Impact	Melee		

Troop name		Type	Armour	Quality	Shooting	Impact	Melee	Points per base	Bases per BG	Total bases
Imperial kürassiere		Determined Horse	Armoured	Average	Carbine	–	Pistol	16	4	4–12
		Determined Horse	Armoured	Average	–	Pistol	Pistol	15	4	
Imperial infantry	Only before 1675	Medium Foot	Unarmoured	Superior	Musket	–	–	11	4	6 — 0–6
		Heavy Foot	Unarmoured	Superior	–	Pike	Pike	8	2	
	Only from 1675	Medium Foot	Unarmoured	Superior	Musket	–	–	11	5	6 — 0–6
		Heavy Foot	Unarmoured	Superior	–	Pike	Pike	8	1	
	Only from 1691	Medium Foot	Unarmoured	Superior	Musket	–	–	10	6	
	Only before 1675	Medium Foot	Unarmoured	Average	Musket	–	–	8	4	6 — 6–24 (6–24)
		Heavy Foot	Unarmoured	Average	–	Pike	Pike	5	2	
		Medium Foot	Unarmoured	Poor	Musket	–	–	6	4	6
		Heavy Foot	Unarmoured	Poor	–	Pike	Pike	3	2	
	Only from 1675	Medium Foot	Unarmoured	Average	Musket	–	–	8	5	6 — 6–24
		Heavy Foot	Unarmoured	Average	–	Pike	Pike	5	1	
		Medium Foot	Unarmoured	Poor	Musket	–	–	6	5	6
		Heavy Foot	Unarmoured	Poor	–	Pike	Pike	3	1	
	Only from 1691	Medium Foot	Unarmoured	Average / Poor	Musket	–	–	7 / 5	6	
3-pdr regimental guns		Regimental Guns	–	Superior	Regimental Guns	Regimental Guns	–	12	n/a	0–1 per Imperial infantry BG
				Average				9		
				Poor				7		
"Spanish riders" or chevaux-de-frise to cover 3 files of each Imperial infantry BG	Only from 1675	Portable Defences						3		Any
Crabaten, Ungaren and, from 1688, regular hussars		Light Horse	Unarmoured	Average	Carbine	–	Pistol	9	4	0–4
Artillery		Heavy Artillery	–	Average	Heavy Artillery	–	–	25	2	0–2
		Medium Artillery	–	Average	Medium Artillery	–	–	20	2	
		Light Artillery	–	Average	Light Artillery	–	–	12	2	

LATER GERMAN STATES

This list covers the armies of the various German states and leagues from the Treaty of Westphalia in 1648 until 1698. The major states are those able to field substantial armies on their own and include, at various times, Bavaria, Saxony, Brandenburg-Prussia and Hanover. Lesser states are those who usually had to ally with other states to field meaningful armies,

such as Hessen-Kassel, Württemberg, Brunswick and the Palatinate. The list also includes the *Reichsarmee* of the Holy Roman Empire, comprised of contingents from a large number of the member states, including Austria itself.

Following the Peace of Westphalia, with many of their lands devastated and depopulated by the armies of various nations in the Thirty Years' War, nearly all of the various German states were quick to disband their armies as a cost saving measure. No doubt they also hoped that these ex-soldiers would return to the land, becoming economically productive as opposed to a drain on finances. Of course, the reality of the international situation meant that it was impossible for the larger states to do without an army in an age where standing armies were coming into being, and within 6 years of the peace being agreed there were at least ten states with a standing force of 1,000 men or more. By 1660 Brandenburg-Prussia had 5,000 men under arms, whilst the Palatinate, Saxony and Bavaria had 3–5,000 each, and all had the capacity

Braunschweig-Lunebergische Truppen

to at least double that in an emergency. In fact Brandenburg-Prussia may have been able to field 18–20,000 men at a push. Even small states such as Pflaz-Neuburg could field 1–2,000 men. To relatively small nations, these standing armies were a considerable financial burden, despite the perceived need for them - for national prestige if nothing else. It therefore became common for states, small and large, to hire out regiments, or occasionally whole armies, to larger richer nations who were in need of additional trained troops at short notice.

In addition to the social and economic effects of the war, the German states also had to come to terms with changes in the political makeup of the Holy Roman Empire. Although, in theory, the rights of the member states, and especially the eight Imperial electors, had been reaffirmed by the Peace of Westphalia, the fact that foreign powers, France and Sweden, were the guarantors of the peace, meant that the Empire's internal politics now had an additional international aspect. However, over the course of the last quarter of the 17th century it became clear that the interests of the German states were, in fact, more closely aligned with the Habsburg monarchy, despite its previous track record of trying to dominate Germany, than with the so-called guarantors of the peace of Westphalia, both of whom had territorial ambitions in Germany. Thus they were more willing than ever to provide contingents for the *Reichsarmee*. Whilst this saw little "front line" action, it did perform useful service tying down French armies in secondary theatres during the War of the League of Augsburg. More practically, it meant that the German states were willing to supply large numbers of men to Austrian armies, especially against the Turks, where their leaders were often appointed to high command and the Austrians provided financial subsidies.

This is not to say that the various German states did not act on their own, or purely in their own interest, during this period. The most ambitious was Brandenburg-Prussia which, under Frederick William, the Great Elector (*Der Grosser Kurfürst*), and his son Frederick, embarked on an expansionist policy, becoming involved in a number of wars in the Baltic region, even beating the vaunted Swedes at the battle of Fehrbellin.

TROOP NOTES

In this period, despite the lessons of the Thirty Years' War, some German horse reverted to the use of firearms as their primary tactic. They do not, however, appear to have also reverted to deep formations, so we continue to classify them as Determined Horse.

From about the end of the 1680s, with the adoption of the bayonet, most German infantry discarded the pike, becoming wholly musketeers. Some of the minor states, however, may have held onto the pike somewhat longer, and so this is optionally allowed in the list.

Saxon infantry, possibly due to their Polish neighbours' cavalry superiority, were equipped

Furst Leopold von Anhalt Dessau Regiment Infantryman

with "Spanish riders", better known to wargamers as Swedish feathers, as additional protection against mounted troops.

BAVARIAN STARTER ARMY (FROM 1689)		
Commander-in-Chief	1	Field Commander
Sub-Commanders	2	2 x Troop Commander
German horse	2 BGs	Each comprising 4 bases of German horse: Average, Armoured Determined Horse – Impact Pistol, Melee Pistol
Bavarian hussars	1 BG	2 bases of Bavarian hussars: Average, Unarmoured, Light Horse – Carbine, Melee Pistol
Guard regiments	1 BG	6 bases of Guard regiments: Superior, Unarmoured Medium Foot – Musket, Bayonet; and Superior Regimental Guns.
German infantry	3 BGs	Each comprising 6 bases of German infantry: Average, Unarmoured Medium Foot – Musket, Bayonet; and Average Regimental Guns.
Dragoons	1 BG	3 bases of Dragoons: Average, Unarmoured Dragoons – Musket
Field artillery	1 BG	2 bases of Field artillery – Average Medium Artillery
Camp	1	Unfortified camp
Total	9 BGs	Camp, 10 mounted bases, 29 foot bases, 3 commanders

BUILDING A CUSTOMISED LIST USING OUR ARMY POINTS

Choose an army based on the maxima and minima in the list below. The following special instructions apply to this army:

• Commanders should be depicted as German horse.

LATER GERMAN STATES									
Territory Types: Agricultural, Woodlands, Hilly									
C-in-C	Great Commander/Field Commander/Troop Commander						80/50/35	1	
Sub-commanders	Field Commander						50	0–2	
	Troop Commander						35	0–3	
Troop name		Troop Type			Capabilities			Points per base	Bases per BG	Total bases
		Type	Armour	Quality	Shooting	Impact	Melee			
Core Troops										
German horse	Bavaria and Saxony at any date, others only before 1689	Determined Horse	Armoured	Average	–	Pistol	Pistol	15	4	4–20
				Poor				11		
		Determined Horse	Armoured	Average	Carbine	–	Pistol	16	4	
				Poor				12		
	Any but Bavaria and Saxony from 1689	Determined Horse	Unarmoured	Average	–	Pistol	Pistol	12	4	
				Poor				9		
		Determined Horse	Unarmoured	Average	Carbine	–	Pistol	13	4	
				Poor				10		
German infantry or militia	Only before 1689 if major state, or any date if lesser state	Medium Foot	Unarmoured	Average	Musket	–	–	8	4	6	18–72
		Heavy Foot	Unarmoured	Average	–	Pike	Pike	5	2	
		Medium Foot	Unarmoured	Poor	Musket	–	–	6	4	6
		Heavy Foot	Unarmoured	Poor	–	Pike	Pike	3	2	
	Only from 1689	Medium Foot	Unarmoured	Average	Musket	Bayonet	Bayonet	9	6	
				Poor				7		
Battalion guns		Regimental Guns	–	Average	Regimental Guns	Regimental Guns	–	9	n/a	0–1 per non–Poor non–light German infantry BG
Light artillery		Light Artillery	–	Average	Light Artillery	–	–	12	2, 3 or 4	2–4
Field artillery		Medium Artillery	–	Average	Medium Artillery	–	–	20	2, 3 or 4	
Optional Troops										
Dragoons		Dragoons	Unarmoured	Average	Musket	–	–	8	3 or 4	0–8
Guard regiments	Only Brandenburg-Prussia before 1689	Medium Foot	Unarmoured	Superior	Musket	–	–	10	6	0–6
	Any other major state before 1689	Medium Foot	Unarmoured	Superior	Musket	–	–	11	4	6
		Heavy Foot	Unarmoured	Superior	–	Pike	Pike	8	2	
	Any major state from 1689	Medium Foot	Unarmoured	Superior	Musket	Bayonet	Bayonet	12	6	

Troop name		Type	Armour	Quality	Shooting	Impact	Melee	Points per base	Bases per BG	Total bases
Battalion guns		Regimental Guns	–	Superior	Regimental Guns	Regimental Guns	–	12	n/a	0–1 per guard regiments BG
Brandenburg-Prussian jaegers	Only Brandenburg-Prussia from 1675	Light Foot	Unarmoured	Average	Musket	–	–	7	4	0–4
Bavarian hussars	Only Bavaria from 1688	Light Horse	Unarmoured	Average	Carbine	–	Pistol	9	2	0–2
"Spanish riders" to cover 3 files of each infantry BG	Only Saxony from 1689	Portable Defences	–	–	–	–	–	3	–	Any
Allies										
Lesser State German allies – Later German States (up to 2 contingents)										
Imperial allies – Habsburg Austrian Imperial										
Polish allies (Only Brandenburg-Prussia from 1657 to 1658 and Saxony from 1687 to 1698) – Later Polish and Lithuanian										

LATER GERMAN STATES ALLIES

Allied commander		Field Commander/Troop Commander						40/25		1
Troop name		**Troop Type**			**Capabilities**			**Points per base**	**Bases per BG**	**Total bases**
		Type	Armour	Quality	Shooting	Impact	Melee			
German horse	Bavaria and Saxony at any date, others only before 1689	Determined Horse	Armoured	Average	–	Pistol	Pistol	15	4	4–12
				Poor				11		
		Determined Horse	Armoured	Average	Carbine	–	Pistol	16	4	
				Poor				12		
	Any but Bavaria and Saxony from 1689	Determined Horse	Unarmoured	Average	–	Pistol	Pistol	12	4	
				Poor				9		
		Determined Horse	Unarmoured	Average	Carbine	–	Pistol	13	4	
				Poor				10		
German infantry or militia	Only before 1689 if major state, or any date if lesser state	Medium Foot	Unarmoured	Average	Musket	–	–	8	4	6
		Heavy Foot	Unarmoured	Average	–	Pike	Pike	5	2	
		Medium Foot	Unarmoured	Poor	Musket	–	–	6	4	6
		Heavy Foot	Unarmoured	Poor	–	Pike	Pike	3	2	
	Only from 1689	Medium Foot	Unarmoured	Average	Musket	Bayonet	Bayonet	9	6	6–30
				Poor				7		
Battalion guns		Regimental Guns	–	Average	Regimental Guns	Regimental Guns	–	9	n/a	0–1 per non-Poor German infantry BG
Light artillery		Light Artillery	–	Average	Light Artillery	–	–	12	2, 3 or 4	0–2
Field artillery		Medium Artillery	–	Average	Medium Artillery	–	–	20	2, 3 or 4	

LATER SPANISH

After more than 100 years of hegemony in Europe, lack of gold from America, financial and political mismanagement by monarchs and regents, and the demographic problem caused by the large numbers of young men sent to war, resulted in the Spanish Empire facing serious financial problems. The Spanish crown declared bankruptcy four times in the 17th century, the last time in 1662. This economic and military decline forced Spain to concede possessions in Flanders and France in the Peace of the Pyrenees in 1659.

The foreign policy of Philip IV of Spain sought peace to preserve the Spanish possessions in Italy, Flanders and Portugal, but military failures, and problems in recruiting and training new soldiers, resulted in a series of territorial losses, especially to France, such as Luxembourg in 1684. The tercios were sometimes reduced to 25 percent of their original number. Philip IV died in 1665 and his wife Marianne assumed the regency during the minority of Charles II. The weakness of the Spanish crown encouraged the Portuguese to fight for their independence, defeating the Spanish armies in the battles of Elvas (1659), Ameixal (1663) and Castelo Rodrigo (1664). Charles II was known as "the Bewitched" because of his physical and mental infirmities. His reign signalled the death knell of the Spanish Empire as a major power, although it would be a long time before it finally disintegrated. Aware of his inability to reign, Charles left the governance of the Empire to a series of regents.

This army list covers Spanish Imperial armies from the Peace of the Pyrenees in 1659 until 1698.

TROOP NOTES

In response to the superiority of the French cavalry, the Imperial cavalry was reorganised in 1649 and 1659 into units of 7–11 companies. Actual strength, however, never approached the theoretical numbers, and the caballos corazas suffered a progressive reduction in Italy and Flanders.

In the campaign in Extremadura against the Portuguese in 1659, the tercios had an actual establishment ranging between 400 and 2,000 men, with the average being 1,000-1,200. A few years later, in 1662, no Spanish tercio numbered more than 600 men, and only a few Italian and German tercios had more than 1,000 men. Even when they contained significant numbers of soldiers, the tercios would usually fight in "battalion" sized formations like other armies of the day. Additionally, the tercios now appear to have fought in formations that were about 6 ranks deep. Because of these factors, and despite the continued use of the name tercio for Spanish regiments, we do not classify any of these battle groups as "Tercios" as defined by the rules.

Some provincial tercios and other infantry regiments were declared inoperative after their recruitment because they did not reach high enough quality to join the army.

12 grenadier companies were created in 1685 and 4 companies of 50 men each were sent to both Flanders and Italy. The remaining 4 were left in Spain. These were, however, attached to existing regiments during field battles, and so do not appear as separate battle groups in this list.

LATER SPANISH STARTER ARMY (IN SPAIN)

Commander-in-Chief	1	Field Commander
Sub-Commanders	2	2 x Troop Commander
Caballos corazos	1 BG	4 bases of Caballos corazos: Superior, Armoured Determined Horse – Impact Pistol, Melee Pistol
Caballos corazos	2 BGs	Each comprising 4 bases of Caballos corazos: Average, Armoured Determined Horse – Impact Pistol, Melee Pistol
Spanish tercios and tercios de las naciones	1 BG	Each comprising 6 bases of Spanish tercios and tercios de las naciones: 4 bases of Average, Unarmoured Medium Foot – Musket; and 2 bases of Average, Armoured Heavy Foot – Pike
Provincial or auxiliary tercios and other foreign regiments	3 BGs	Each comprising 6 bases of Provincial or auxiliary tercios and other foreign regiments: 4 bases of Average, Unarmoured Medium Foot – Musket; and 2 bases of Average, Unarmoured Heavy Foot – Pike
Miquelets	1 BG	6 bases of Miquelets: Average, Unarmoured Light Foot – Musket
Dragoons	1 BG	3 bases of Dragoons: Average, Unarmoured Dragoons – Musket
Field guns	1 BG	2 bases of Field guns – Average Medium Artillery
Camp	1	Unfortified camp
Total	10 BGs	Camp, 12 mounted bases, 35 foot bases, 3 commanders

BUILDING A CUSTOMISED LIST USING OUR ARMY POINTS

Choose an army based on the maxima and minima in the list below. The following special instructions apply to this army:

- Commanders should be depicted as caballos corazas.
- No more than half the battle groups of caballos corazas fielded can be Superior.

LATER SPANISH

Territory Types: Agricultural

C-in-C	Great Commander/Field Commander/Troop Commander						80/50/35		1	
Sub-commanders	Field Commander						50		0–2	
	Troop Commander						35		0–3	

Troop name	Troop Type			Capabilities			Points per base	Bases perBG	Total bases
	Type	Armour	Quality	Shooting	Impact	Melee			
Core Troops									
Caballos corazos	Determined Horse	Armoured	Superior	–	Pistol	Pistol	21	4	4–16 in Spain, 4–12 in Flanders, 0–8 in Italy
			Average				15		
Spanish tercios and tercios de las naciones	Medium Foot	Unarmoured	Average	Musket	–	–	8	4	6	6–60
	Heavy Foot	Armoured	Average	–	Pike	Pike	6	2	
Provincial or auxiliary tercios and other foreign regiments	Medium Foot	Unarmoured	Average	Musket	–	–	8	4	6	12–60 in Spain, 0–24 in Flanders or Italy
	Heavy Foot	Unarmoured	Average	–	Pike	Pike	5	2	
	Medium Foot	Unarmoured	Poor	Musket	–	–	6	4	6	
	Heavy Foot	Unarmoured	Poor	–	Pike	Pike	3	2	
Tercios Viejos Españoles — Only in Flanders or Italy	Medium Foot	Unarmoured	Superior	Musket	–	–	11	4	6	0–12
	Heavy Foot	Armoured	Superior	–	Pike	Pike	9	2	

Field guns		Medium Artillery	–	Average	Medium Artillery	–	–	20	2, 3 or 4	0–6
Heavy guns		Heavy Artillery	–	Average	Heavy Artillery	–	–	25	2	
Optional Troops										
Arquebusiers		Horse	Unarmoured	Average	Carbine	–	Pistol	9	4	0–8
Dragoons	Any date in Spain or Italy	Dragoons	Unarmoured	Average	Musket	–	–	8	3 or 4	0–8
	Only from 1674 in Flanders									
Miquelets	Only in Spain	Light Foot	Unarmoured	Average	Musket	–	–	7	6–8	0–12
German infantry	Only in Flanders from 1689	Medium Foot	Unarmoured	Average	Musket	Bayonet	Bayonet	9	6	0–18
Allies										
Dutch allies (Only from 1683) – Later Dutch										
Anglo–Dutch allies (Only from 1689) – War of the League of Augsburg Anglo-Dutch										
Savoyard allies (Only in Italy from 1689) – Savoyard										

LATER SPANISH ALLIES

Allied commander		Field Commander/Troop Commander						40/25		1
Troop name		**Troop Type**			**Capabilities**			**Points per base**	**Bases per BG**	**Total bases**
		Type	Armour	Quality	Shooting	Impact	Melee			
Caballos corazas		Determined Horse	Armoured	Superior	–	Pistol	Pistol	21	4	4–8 in Spain or Flanders, 0–4 in Italy
				Average				15		
Spanish tercios and tercios de las naciones		Medium Foot	Unarmoured	Average	Musket	–	–	8	4	6–24
		Heavy Foot	Armoured	Average	–	Pike	Pike	6	2	
Provincial or auxiliary tercios and other foreign regiments		Medium Foot	Unarmoured	Average	Musket	–	–	8	4	6–24 in Spain, 0–12 in Flanders or Italy
		Heavy Foot	Unarmoured	Average	–	Pike	Pike	5	2	
		Medium Foot	Unarmoured	Poor	Musket	–	–	6	4	
		Heavy Foot	Unarmoured	Poor	–	Pike	Pike	3	2	
Tercios Viejos Españoles	Only in Flanders or Italy	Medium Foot	Unarmoured	Superior	Musket	–	–	11	4	0–6
		Heavy Foot	Armoured	Superior	–	Pike	Pike	9	2	
Field guns		Medium Artillery	–	Average	Medium Artillery	–	–	20	2	0–2
Heavy guns		Heavy Artillery	–	Average	Heavy Artillery	–	–	25	2	

LATER RESTORATION PORTUGUESE

*O*n 1 December 1640, a small group of conspirators assaulted Lisbon and deposed Spanish rule. The Duke of Braganza was crowned as Joao IV of Portugal, vowing to fight for independence against the Spanish. The Spanish counter attack, organized by the "Inquisición", began the Portuguese Restoration War, which was to last 28 years and end with the recognition of Portuguese independence in the Peace of Lisbon.

The Spanish were also occupied in war against France until the peace of the Pyrenees in 1659, after which they launched an offensive and besieged Elvas. A relief army commanded by the Count of Cantanhede defeated the Spanish and freed the city. A year later, the Portuguese Queen Regent signed an agreement with the restored Stuart monarchy allowing the Portuguese to recruit troops in Britain. After this, the Count of Castelo Melhor began an offensive in the south to defeat the Spanish army of Extremadura. The Portuguese won the battles of Ameixial in 1663 and Castelo Rodrigo in 1664. Finally, in 1665, the Portuguese defeated the Imperial army at the battle of Montes Claros. Charles II gave up the fight and the Peace of Lisbon was signed in 1668.

This list covers Portuguese armies from 1660 to 1698.

TROOP NOTES

Portuguese infantry had adopted Spanish fighting methods while under Imperial rule. Tercios were called Terços in Portugal – initially 4 were created: Lisbon, Estremadura, Alentejo and Algarve. These were soon supplemented by additional terços and foreign infantry regiments. As with the

Spanish, the Portuguese carried on equipping their front line units with pikemen's armour throughout this period, but this was not the case with the auxiliary and militia units.

A Terço of Marines was created in 1621 – this unit was the origin of the present-day Portuguese Marines, and was considered an elite guard.

The British provided a regular supply of troops, mainly infantry, to support the Portuguese in their struggle against Spain. As they appear to have been more or less integrated into the Portuguese army, we do not consider that they should be represented by an allied contingent.

British Cavalry

LATER RESTORATION PORTUGUESE STARTER ARMY

Commander-in-Chief	1	Field Commander
Sub-Commanders	2	2 x Troop Commander
Cavalos couraças	2 BGs	Each comprising 4 bases of Cavalos couraças: Average, Armoured Determined Horse – Impact Pistol, Melee Pistol
Arcabuzeiros a cavalo	2 BGs	Each comprising 4 bases of Arcabuzeiros a cavalo: Average, Unarmoured Horse – Carbine, Melee Pistol
Terços	1 BG	6 bases of Terços: 4 bases of Average, Unarmoured Medium Foot – Musket; 2 bases of Average, Armoured Heavy Foot – Pike
Auxiliary or militia terços and other regiments, and foreign mercenaries	4 BGs	Each comprising 6 bases of Auxiliary or militia terços and other regiments, and foreign mercenaries: 4 bases of Average, Unarmoured Medium Foot – Musket; 2 bases of Average, Unarmoured Heavy Foot – Pike
Fuzileiros	1 BG	4 bases of Average, Unarmoured Medium Foot – Musket, Bayonet
Field guns	1 BG	2 bases of Field guns – Average Medium Artillery
Camp	1	Unfortified camp
Total	11 BGs	Camp, 16 mounted bases, 36 foot bases, 3 commanders

BUILDING A CUSTOMISED LIST USING OUR ARMY POINTS

Choose an army based on the maxima and minima in the list below. The following special instructions apply to this army:

• Commanders should be depicted as cavalos couraças.

LATER RESTORATION PORTUGUESE

Territory Types: Agricultural

Troop name	Troop Type		Capabilities			Points per base	Bases per BG	Total bases
C-in-C	Great Commander/Field Commander/Troop Commander					80/50/35	1	
Sub-commanders	Field Commander					50	0-2	
	Troop Commander					35	0-3	
Troop name	Type	Armour	Quality	Shooting	Impact	Melee		

Troop name	Type	Armour	Quality	Shooting	Impact	Melee	Points per base	Bases per BG	Total bases
Core Troops									
Cavalos couraças	Determined Horse	Armoured	Average	-	Pistol	Pistol	15	4	4-12
Arcabuzeiros a cavalo	Horse	Unarmoured	Average	Carbine	-	Pistol	9	4	0-8
Terços	Medium Foot	Unarmoured	Average	Musket	-	-	8	4	6	6-36
	Heavy Foot	Armoured	Average	-	Pike	Pike	6	2		
Auxiliary or militia terços and other regiments, and foreign mercenaries	Medium Foot	Unarmoured	Average	Musket	-	-	8	4	6	18-60
	Heavy Foot	Unarmoured	Average	-	Pike	Pike	5	2		
	Medium Foot	Unarmoured	Poor	Musket	-	-	6	4	6	
	Heavy Foot	Unarmoured	Poor	-	Pike	Pike	3	2		
Field guns	Medium Artillery	-	Average	Medium Artillery	-	-	20	2, 3 or 4	0-4
Light guns	Light Artillery	-	Average	Light Artillery	-	-	12	2, 3 or 4	

Optional Troops											
Terço of marines and veterans		Medium Foot	Unarmoured	Superior	Musket	-	-	11	4	6	0-6
		Heavy Foot	Armoured	Superior	-	Pike	Pike	9	2		
Fuzileiros		Medium foot	Unarmoured	Average	Musket	Bayonet	Bayonet	9	4-6		0-6
British horse		Determined Horse	Armoured	Average	-	Pistol	Pistol	15	4		0-4
British foot	Only before 1678	Medium Foot	Unarmoured	Average	Musket	-	-	8	4	6	
		Heavy Foot	Armoured	Average	-	Pike	Pike	6	2		
	Only from 1678 to 1688	Medium Foot	Unarmoured	Average	Musket	-	-	8	4	6	0-18
		Heavy Foot	Unarmoured	Average	-	Pike	Pike	5	2		
	Only from 1689	Medium Foot	Unarmoured	Average	Musket	Bayonet	Bayonet	8	5	6	
		Heavy Foot	Unarmoured	Average	-	Pike	Pike	5	1		
Fortifications		Field Fortifications	-	-	-	-	-	3	-		0-12

SAVOYARD

This list covers the armies of Savoy from 1649 to 1698.

For the majority of the period the Duchy of Savoy stayed out of the wars of the great powers. Before the War of the League of Augsburg, it had only been engaged in one small conflict, the Second Genoese-Savoyard War, where Savoy attacked Genoese possessions. However, there was no fighting of any consequence, and the war ended less than a year after it had begun.

During the War of the League of Augsburg, Savoy joined the Grand Alliance opposing Louis XIV. This brought a French army under Catinat, one of Louis' better generals, into the country, where it promptly defeated the Savoyard army. The Duchy was bolstered by military aid from the Spanish and Austrians, the latter, oddly enough, under the command of Prince Eugene of Savoy, cousin of the Duke of Savoy, Victor Amadeus II. With the French concentrating on the Rhine theatre of war, Savoy was able to recover and take the offensive against France's possessions in the area, attempting to capture Pinerolo. Unfortunately Catinat returned to relieve the city, and again crushingly defeated the Savoyard-Spanish army at the Battle of Marsaglia, inflicting around 10,000 casualties for the loss of only 1,000 Frenchmen. Despite this defeat, Savoy remained in the war, partly because again France was in no position to press on. This tenacity paid dividends for Victor Amadeus, as in 1696, as part of a diplomatic strategy to break the Grand Alliance, Louis made peace with Savoy and gave up all his gains in the area, plus the town of Pinerolo.

TROOP NOTES

Savoy relied heavily on foreign troops for its infantry. Whilst many of these were recruited directly as mercenaries, mainly Swiss and German, the Duke also received aid from his allies, in the form of units from their armies. On occasion they supplied large contingents, which are treated as allies.

For example, during the War of the League of Augsburg, the Spanish supplied troops from their Italian possessions to support Savoy in its fight against France. The number of these varied between a few regiments and substantial contingents. We represent the former as battle groups within the Savoyard army, and the latter as an allied contingent.

Savoy had been one of the refuges to which Huguenots had fled during Louis XIV's persecutions and enforced conversions of the early 1680s. In 1691 a number of volunteer regiments were formed from these refugees to fight against France. Ironically, considering the role of dragoons

in causing the Huguenots to flee France, this included a dragoon regiment. It is possible that the infantry had the same "press on" attitude as their compatriots in Louis' armies, and so we allow them the same classification in this list.

In 1693 Savoy received a number of infantry regiments, including guards, from the Elector of Bavaria.

SAVOYARD STARTER ARMY (FROM 1685)		
Commander-in-Chief	1	Field Commander
Sub-Commanders	2	2 x Troop Commander
Savoyard horse	4 BGs	Each comprising 4 bases of Savoyard horse: Average, Unarmoured Determined Horse – Impact Pistol, Melee Pistol
Savoyard guard infantry	1 BG	6 bases of Savoyard guard infantry: 5 bases of Superior, Unarmoured Medium Foot – Musket, Bayonet; and 1 base of Superior, Unarmoured Heavy Foot – Pike
Savoyard, mercenary or militia infantry	3 BGs	Each comprising 6 bases of Savoyard, mercenary or militia infantry: 5 bases of Average, Unarmoured Medium Foot – Musket, Bayonet; and 1 base of Average, Unarmoured Heavy Foot – Pike
Huguenot refugee foot	1 BG	6 bases of Huguenot refugee foot: 5 bases of Average, Unarmoured Medium Foot – Musket*, Impact Foot, Bayonet; and 1 base of Average, Unarmoured Heavy Foot – Pike
Field artillery	1 BG	2 bases of Field artillery – Average Medium Artillery
Camp	1	Unfortified camp
Total	10 BGs	Camp, 16 mounted bases, 32 foot bases, 3 commanders

BUILDING A CUSTOMISED LIST USING OUR ARMY POINTS

Choose an army based on the maxima and minima in the list below. The following special instructions apply to this army:

• Commanders should be depicted as Savoyard horse.
• The Spanish infantry in the Optional Troops section cannot be fielded if Spanish allies are used.

SAVOYARD								
Territory Types: Agricultural, Woodlands, Hilly								
C-in-C	Great Commander/Field Commander/Troop Commander					80/50/35	1	
Sub-commanders	Field Commander					50	0–2	
	Troop Commander					35	0–3	

Troop name	Troop Type			Capabilities			Points per base	Bases BG	Total bases
	Type	Armour	Quality	Shooting	Impact	Melee			
Core Troops									
Savoyard horse	Determined Horse	Unarmoured	Average	–	Pistol	Pistol	12	4	4–20
			Poor				9		
Savoyard, mercenary or militia infantry	Only before 1685	Medium Foot	Unarmoured	Average	Musket	–	–	8	4	6	18–102
		Heavy Foot	Unarmoured	Average	–	Pike	Pike	5	2	
		Medium Foot	Unarmoured	Poor	Musket	–	–	6	4	6
		Heavy Foot	Unarmoured	Poor	–	Pike	Pike	3	2	
	Only from 1685	Medium Foot	Unarmoured	Average	Musket	Bayonet	Bayonet	8	5	6
		Heavy Foot	Unarmoured	Average	–	Pike	Pike	5	1	
		Medium Foot	Unarmoured	Poor	Musket	Bayonet	Bayonet	6	5	6
		Heavy Foot	Unarmoured	Poor	–	Pike	Pike	3	1	
Light artillery	Light Artillery	–	Average	Light Artillery			12	2, 3 or 4	2–4
Field artillery	Medium Artillery	–	Average	Medium Artillery			20	2, 3 or 4	
Optional Troops									
Savoyard guard infantry	Only before 1685	Medium Foot	Unarmoured	Superior	Musket	–	–	11	4	6	0–6
		Heavy Foot	Unarmoured	Superior	–	Pike	Pike	8	2	
	Only from 1685	Medium Foot	Unarmoured	Superior	Musket	Bayonet	Bayonet	11	5	6
		Heavy Foot	Unarmoured	Superior	–	Pike	Pike	8	1	
Dragoons	Dragoons	Unarmoured	Average	Musket	–	–	8	3 or 4	0–8
Huguenot refugee foot	Only from 1691	Medium Foot	Unarmoured	Average	Musket*	Impact Foot + Bayonet	Bayonet	8	5	6	0–18
		Heavy Foot	Unarmoured	Average	–	Pike	Pike	5	1	
Spanish infantry	Only from 1689	Medium Foot	Unarmoured	Average	Musket	–	–	8	4	6	0–12
		Heavy Foot	Unarmoured	Average	–	Pike	Pike	5	2	
Bavarian guards	Only from 1693	Medium Foot	Unarmoured	Superior	Musket	Bayonet	Bayonet	12	6	0–6
Bavarian infantry		Medium Foot	Unarmoured	Average	Musket	Bayonet	Bayonet	9	6	0–12
Allies									
Spanish allies – Later Spanish (Italian options)									
Imperial allies (Only from 1689) – Habsburg Austrian Imperial									
Brandenburg-Prussian allies (Only in 1694) – Later German States									

SAVOYARD ALLIES									
Allied commander	Field Commander/Troop Commander						40/25	1	
Troop name	Troop Type			Capabilities			Points per base	Bases per BG	Total bases
	Type	Armour	Quality	Shooting	Impact	Melee			
Savoyard horse	Determined Horse	Unarmoured	Average	–	Pistol	Pistol	12	4	4–8
			Poor				9		
Savoyard, mercenary or militia infantry	Medium Foot	Unarmoured	Average	Musket	Bayonet	Bayonet	8	5	6
	Heavy Foot	Unarmoured	Average	–	Pike	Pike	5	1	6–36
	Medium Foot	Unarmoured	Poor	Musket	Bayonet	Bayonet	6	5	6
	Heavy Foot	Unarmoured	Poor	–	Pike	Pike	3	1	
Light artillery	Light Artillery	–	Average	Light Artillery	–	–	12	2	0–2
Field artillery	Medium Artillery	–	Average	Medium Artillery	–	–	20	2	

RESTORATION BRITISH

This list covers the armies of Charles II and his brother James II from Charles' restoration to the crown in 1660 until James' overthrow by the "Glorious Revolution" of 1688 that brought William III to the English throne. Although mainly covering the English armies, the list also includes the small Scottish army until 1690, and the army in Ireland.

With the collapse of the Commonwealth following Oliver Cromwell's death and the lacklustre performance of his son Richard, Parliament invited Charles I's son to take the throne as Charles II. At the same time he became King of Scotland and King of Ireland, although

British Infantry

*The King's Royal Regiment of Foot Guards, 1685, by Angus McBride © Osprey Publishing Ltd.
Taken from Men-at-Arms 73:* The Grenadier Guards.

he had previously been crowned in Scotland in 1651 at Scone.

As part of the restoration, the army, which had been the instrument by which the Commonwealth had been maintained, was drastically reduced in size so that it would no longer be a political threat. There was now an inherent distrust of standing armies amongst the ruling classes. Additionally, it was now officered by monarchy friendly "Cavaliers" rather than those who might oppose the monarchy. However, it was soon found that the vastly reduced army was too small even for the limited military needs of the kingdoms, and there was a steady increase in its establishment throughout

Charles' and James' reigns, although the army remained small compared to those of some of its continental contemporaries, such as France and the United Provinces.

Charles II's marriage, in 1662, to the Portuguese princess Catherine of Braganza, brought overseas territories in Tangiers and Mumbai as her dowry. These required garrisons, leading to a continual need for troops to be sent overseas, although this was partly offset by the sale of Dunkirk to Louis XIV. In general, however, the army saw little activity in Charles' reign, with the wars with the Dutch being naval affairs, although a few troops were sent to aid Louis XIV from 1672 to 1674.

Charles was succeeded by his brother James, whose reign is mostly remembered for the Monmouth rebellion, which was suppressed, and the "Glorious Revolution" which cost James his thrones. Both were caused by James' Catholic faith,

Matchlockmen at Sedgemoor, 1685, by Stephen Walsh © Osprey Publishing Ltd.
Taken from Warrior 43: Matchlock Musketeer.

RESTORATION BRITISH

which was at best distrusted by the majority in England and Scotland, although it was popular with the Catholic Irish. In his short reign James continued to expand the army which, if he had held his nerve in 1688 when William III landed, would have probably fought for him despite the unpopularity of his religion. Unfortunately for James, the desertion of a number of senior officers to William convinced him that England was lost, and he fled to France. This allowed the English parliament to deem that he had abdicated, paving the way for William's peaceful accession in England.

TROOP NOTES

Although guard regiments of both horse and foot formed the core of the standing army of the period, lack of military activity suggests that they were unlikely to be better in action than any of the line regiments. Thus we do not rate them as anything other than Average. However, they, along with the newly created Fusiliers, were the first infantry regiments outside the Tangier garrison to be issued with bayonets, starting in 1686.

The horse of the Restoration army was equipped, and fought, more or less as that of the Commonwealth army. The main difference would

be that over time the three-barred helmet of the civil war period was replaced by an iron skull cap, or "secret", worn under a brimmed hat.

With the large scale reduction of the army inherited from the Commonwealth, it was once again practical for pikemen to be issued with corselets, although this may not have been universal. Additionally, lack of long arduous campaigns removed the incentive to discard the armour to make life on the march easier. One exception to this appears to have been the Tangiers garrison, where the climatic conditions would have made wearing armour difficult for English soldiers. With the steadily increasing size of the army throughout the two reigns, however, and especially in that of James, it appears that once again pikemen's armour was discarded by, or never issued to, many regiments.

The first regiment of dragoons raised for the Restoration army was created in 1672 as Prince Rupert's Regiment of Dragoons, although it was soon disbanded. Dragoons were again raised from 1678.

During this period the Scottish army was nominally independent of its English counterpart but served alongside it on the Continent.

British Dragoons

English units were part of the army, but are not treated as allies as in practice they served under the same command structure and were brigaded with Scots units.

At the time of the accession of William III to the throne, the entire Scottish army was in England. William was extremely doubtful of their loyalty and sent the whole force, with the exception of the Scots Greys, to the continent to fight the French. The Scots Greys were sent back to Scotland, where they came close to mutiny but held to their allegiance.

When Dundee raised the Highlands in support of James, a whole new army had to be raised from scratch for William, although, unlike in England, the units were all volunteers and not the product of a fencible or militia system. Not surprisingly, the results were mixed, with some units being poor but most performing well, particularly the Earl of Angus' regiment, which held Dunkeld against the entire Highland army. This unit of ex-Covenanters eventually became the "Cameronians." William

sent the veteran Dutch Brigade of Scottish mercenaries to support the Scottish army but, despite its veteran status, it does not appear to have performed any better than the rest of the army.

Many Scottish units in the Killiekrankie campaign (1689) appear to have had few, if any, pikes. One view is that this was an equipment shortage, but it is also likely that pikes were of limited value, owing to the opposition's shortage of horse, and firelocks were maximised as a preferable alternative. Regular units were often accompanied by small bodies of native Highlanders with traditional weaponry. Although these were better supplied with muskets than clan formations, we still rate them as Musket*, Impact Foot because we assume that they retained the usual Highland enthusiasm for close combat. Owing to the nature of Highland terrain, and the lack of roads, artillery was difficult to move, and was used in only limited numbers. At Killiekrankie, Mackay's guns consisted of a few light pieces, most of which collapsed after a few rounds.

RESTORATION BRITISH STARTER ARMY (FROM 1685)		
Commander-in-Chief	1	Field Commander
Sub-Commanders	2	2 x Troop Commander
Guards and other horse regiments	3 BGs	Each comprising 4 bases of Guards and other horse regiments: Average, Armoured Determined Horse – Impact Pistol, Melee Pistol
Newly recruited or militia horse	1 BG	4 bases of Newly recruited or militia horse: Average, Unarmoured Determined Horse – Impact Pistol, Melee Pistol
Foot guards	2 BGs	Each comprising 6 bases of Foot guards: 4 bases of Average, Unarmoured Medium Foot – Musket, Bayonet; and 2 bases of Average, Armoured Heavy Foot – Pike
Other infantry regiments	2 BGs	Each comprising 6 bases of Other infantry regiments: 4 bases of Average, Unarmoured Medium Foot – Musket; and 2 bases of Average, Unarmoured Heavy Foot – Pike
Dragoons	1 BG	4 bases of Dragoons: Average, Unarmoured Dragoons – Musket
Field artillery	1 BG	2 bases of Field artillery – Average Medium Artillery
Camp	1	Unfortified camp
Total	10 BGs	Camp, 16 mounted bases, 30 foot bases, 3 commanders

English Cavalry in Tangiers, 1680, by Graham Turner © Osprey Publishing Ltd. Taken from Warrior 44: Ironsides.

BUILDING A CUSTOMISED LIST USING OUR ARMY POINTS

Choose an army based on the maxima and minima in the list below. The following special instructions apply to this army:

- Commanders should be depicted as mounted guards.
- The minima marked * does not apply to the Tangiers garrison nor in Scotland from 1670 to 1690 (Special Campaign).

RESTORATION BRITISH									
Territory Types: Agricultural, Hilly, Woodlands									
C-in-C	Great Commander/Field Commander/Troop Commander						80/50/35	1	
Sub-commanders	Field Commander						50	0–2	
	Troop Commander						35	0–3	
Troop name	Troop Type			Capabilities			Points per base	Bases per BG	Total bases
	Type	Armour	Quality	Shooting	Impact	Melee			
Core Troops									
Guards and other horse regiments	Determined Horse	Armoured	Average	–	Pistol	Pistol	15	4	*8–24
Foot guards	Only before 1686	Medium Foot	Unarmoured	Average	Musket	–	–	8	4	6	0–18
		Heavy Foot	Armoured	Average	–	Pike	Pike	6	2	
	Only from 1686	Medium Foot	Unarmoured	Average	Musket	Bayonet	Bayonet	8	4	6
		Heavy Foot	Armoured	Average	–	Pike	Pike	6	2	
Other infantry regiments	Only before 1678	Medium Foot	Unarmoured	Average	Musket	–	–	8	4	6	12–84	12–84
		Heavy Foot	Armoured	Average	–	Pike	Pike	6	2	
		Medium Foot	Unarmoured	Average	Musket	–	–	8	4	6	0–30
		Heavy Foot	Unarmoured	Average	–	Pike	Pike	5	2	
	Only from 1678	Medium Foot	Unarmoured	Average	Musket	–	–	8	4	6	12–84
		Heavy Foot	Unarmoured	Average	–	Pike	Pike	5	2	
3-pdr battalion guns	Only from 1686	Regimental Guns	–	Average	Regimental Guns	Regimental Guns	–	9	n/a	0-1 per foot guards or other infantry regiments BG
Field artillery		Medium Artillery	–	Average	Medium Artillery	–	–	20	2, 3 or 4	0–4	*2–4
Light artillery		Light Artillery	–	Average	Light Artillery	–	–	12	2	0–2
Optional Troops									
Dragoons	Only in 1672	Dragoons	Unarmoured	Average	Musket	–	–	8	3 or 4	0–4
	Only from 1678									0–6
Fusiliers	Only from 1686	Medium Foot	Unarmoured	Average	Musket	Bayonet	Bayonet	9	4–6	0–6

RESTORATION BRITISH

Troop name	Type	Armour	Quality	Shooting	Impact	Melee	Points per base	Bases per BG	Total bases
Newly recruited or militia horse	Determined Horse	Unarmoured	Average / Poor	–	Pistol	Pistol	12 / 9	4	0–8
Newly recruited or militia foot	Medium Foot	Unarmoured	Poor	Musket	–	–	6	4	6	0–48
	Heavy Foot	Unarmoured	Poor	–	Pike	Pike	3	2	

Special Campaigns									

Tangiers garrison, 1662 to 1684

No more than 3 BGs of horse may be fielded and no newly raised or militia troops can be used. Guards and other infantry regiments are replaced by Tangiers garrison infantry below.

	Type	Armour	Quality	Shooting	Impact	Melee	Points per base	Bases per BG	Total bases
Tangiers garrison infantry	Medium Foot	Unarmoured	Average	Musket	Bayonet	Bayonet	8	4	6	24–120
	Heavy Foot	Unarmoured	Average	–	Pike	Pike	5	2	
Spanish mercenary horse — Only from 1680	Determined Horse	Armoured	Average	–	Pistol	Pistol	15	4	0–4
		Unarmoured					12		
Fortifications	Field Fortifications	–	–	–	–	–	3	–	0–12

In Scotland, 1670 to 1690

No Foot Guards or Field Artillery may be fielded, and at least 18 bases of Newly recruited foot must be used. A maximum of 3 battle groups of mounted can be fielded.

	Type	Armour	Quality	Shooting	Impact	Melee	Points per base	Bases per BG	Total bases
Highland scout companies	Warriors	Unarmoured	Average	Musket*	Impact Foot	Swordsmen	8	4–6	0–8
Earl of Angus's regiment	Medium Foot	Unarmoured	Superior	Musket	–	–	11	4	6	0–6
	Heavy Foot	Unarmoured	Superior	–	Pike	Pike	8	2	
Poor quality cavalry regiments	Determined Horse	Armoured	Poor	–	Pistol	Pistol	11	4	0–12
Replace other infantry regiments or newly recruited foot with all shot regiments	Medium Foot	Unarmoured	Average	Musket	–	–	7	6	0–36
			Poor				5		

RESTORATION BRITISH ALLIES

Allied commander	Field Commander/Troop Commander						40/25	1	
Troop name	**Troop Type**			**Capabilities**			**Points per base**	**Bases per BG**	**Total bases**
	Type	Armour	Quality	Shooting	Impact	Melee			
Guards and other horse regiments	Determined Horse	Armoured	Average	–	Pistol	Pistol	15	4	4–8
Other infantry regiments	Medium Foot	Unarmoured	Average	Musket	–	–	8	4	6	6–24
	Heavy Foot	Armoured	Average	–	Pike	Pike	6	2		
	Medium Foot	Unarmoured	Average	Musket	–	–	8	4	6	0–18	6–24
	Heavy Foot	Unarmoured	Average	–	Pike	Pike	5	2		
Newly recruited or militia foot	Medium Foot	Unarmoured	Poor	Musket	–	–	6	4	6	0–18
	Heavy Foot	Unarmoured	Poor	–	Pike	Pike	3	2	
Field artillery	Medium Artillery	–	Average	Medium Artillery	–	–	20	2	0–2
Light artillery	Light Artillery	–	Average	Light Artillery	–	–	12	2	

Trooper of the King's Troop of Horse Guards breaking up a fight between a pikeman of the Coldstream Regiment of Foot Guards and a musketeer of Lord Wentworth's Foot Guards, 1661, by Gerry Embleton © Osprey Publishing Ltd. Taken from Men-at-Arms 267: The British Army 1660–1704.

COVENANTING REBELS

This list covers the forces raised by the Scottish Covenanting rebels in "The Killing Times," encompassing the period from 1670 to the "Glorious Revolution" of 1689.

With his restoration to the British throne, Charles II was determined to take his revenge on those he considered responsible for the execution of his father. In Scotland his principal target was Montrose's old nemesis, Archibald Campbell, Earl of Argyll, whom he considered the Scot most responsible for handing his father over to the English parliament. Argyll was executed in Edinburgh on the Maiden, an early form of guillotine.

Charles also sought revenge on the supporters of the Solemn League and Covenant, whose basic form of religion did not tie in with his more "high church" view.

He therefore ordered the Presbyterian clergy to swear allegiance to newly appointed bishops and to himself. This demand flew in the face of the beliefs of the Covenanters, who would have no king but Jesus. As a result, nearly a quarter of the Scottish clergy locked up their churches and took to the hills. From now on they would preach to their flocks in the open air, often using a large stone as a pulpit. These conventicles were recorded as having congregations as high as 10,000. The gatherings also took on the appearance of small armies, as many men came armed.

Faced with this rebellion, Charles ordered his army in Scotland to put down the movement and arrest the ringleaders. This period became known as the "Killing Times", as many individuals and groups were executed or just cut down by Government enforcers. In truth, the number of dead was relatively small, and the Covenanters were not against exacting some retribution themselves – such as when they murdered the Archbishop of St Andrews after dragging him from his coach. Many Covenanters also seemed to seek death – such as James Renwick. As a young man, he had been taken by his mother to the execution of several Covenanters and, as a result, decided that martyrdom was the career path for him. He thereafter seemed to go out of his way to fulfil his ambition, until the government executed him in 1688 for exchanging shots with government troops in the heart of Edinburgh.

Other than an abortive attempt by a large Covenanting force to march on Edinburgh, the first action took place at Drumclog in 1679. John Graham of Claverhouse (soon to be immortalized as Bonnie Dundee, but already known by the Covenanters as "Bluidy Clavers" as

Covenanting Rebels

a result of his enforcement activities in Scotland) decided to break up a large Covenanting meeting. One eyewitness recorded them as being some 9,000 strong. Graham, in a manner reminiscent of Custer at the Little Big Horn some 200 years later, appeared to be more concerned about the Covenanters escaping than what would happen if they resisted. Graham had in fact only 120 dragoons, but seemed buoyed by the fact that in the approach to Drumclog a handful of dragoons in skirmish order had dispersed a battalion of Covenanters. The main body of Covenanters surged forward singing psalms. Graham at this point appears to have realised the serious position he was in, and tried to negotiate. The Covenanters were, however, in no mood for compromise, and in the brief action that ensued the dragoons were put to rout. Graham escaped with his life, although his standard bearer was virtually torn limb from limb when the Covenanters mistook him for Graham. While government losses were only ten killed, the victory inspired the Covenanters, who began to gather in even larger numbers.

Panicked by Graham's defeat, the parliament in Edinburgh gathered a larger army, and the Duke of Monmouth, soon to launch a rebellion himself, arrived to take command. The Covenanters were found in significant numbers near Bothwell Bridge, and, after a battle of several hours, were dispersed by the government forces. Many prisoners were taken and executions followed.

No other major actions took place, but the Covenanting movement remained alive until the more acceptable monarchy of William and Mary.

TROOP NOTES

Whilst untrained and undisciplined, the Covenanters, inspired by their original fervour, made difficult foes. A famous Scottish actor recently made a serious statement comparing the Covenanters with the Taliban, and it is easy to see the validity of this view when one considers their unswerving commitment to their religion, and the lengths they would go to in defence of it.

Although, in terms of training and equipment, many of the bodies involved in the clashes would be little better than mobs of indifferent quality, bodies of troops with firearms and even fairly substantial bodies of cavalry are recorded. As time progressed, more and more worshippers came to the meetings armed with weapons.

A limited number of sub-commanders are allowed as different factions often did not cooperate well, even in the heat of battle.

Covenanting Cavalry

COVENANTING REBELS

COVENANTING REBELS STARTER ARMY

Commander-in-Chief	1	Troop Commander
Sub-Commanders	2	2 x Troop Commander
Cavalry	2 BGs	Each comprising 4 bases of Cavalry: Average, Unarmoured Horse – Impact Pistol, Swordsmen
Devoted male worshippers	1 BG	12 bases of Devoted male worshippers: Average, Unarmoured Warriors – Heavy Weapon
Devoted male worshippers	1 BG	10 bases of Devoted male worshippers: Average, Unarmoured Warriors – Heavy Weapon
Devoted male worshippers	2 BGs	Each comprising 10 bases of Devoted male worshippers: Average, Unarmoured Mob
Well-armed devoted male worshippers	3 BGs	Each comprising 6 bases of Well-armed devoted male worshippers: Average, Unarmoured Warriors – Musket*
Well-armed devoted male worshippers	2 BGs	Each comprising 6 bases of Well-armed devoted male worshippers: Average, Unarmoured Light Foot – Musket
Infirm, women and children	2 BGs	Each comprising 12 bases of Infirm, women and children: Poor, Unarmoured Mob
Camp	1	Unfortified camp
Total	13 BGs	Camp, 8 mounted bases, 96 foot bases, 3 commanders

BUILDING A CUSTOMISED LIST USING OUR ARMY POINTS

Choose an army based on the maxima and minima in the list below. The following special instructions apply to this army:

- Commanders should be depicted as cavalry or as a debating mob led by a minister.
- There must be at least as many battle groups of Devoted male worshippers with no impact or melee capabilities as there are with Heavy Weapon capability.

COVENANTING REBELS

Territory Types: Agricultural, Woodland, Hilly

C-in-C	Great Commander/Field Commander/Troop Commander						80/50/35	1	
Sub-commanders	Field/Troop Commander						50/35	0–2	
Allied commanders	Field/Troop Commander						40/25	0–3	
Troop name	Troop Type			Capabilities			Points per base	Bases per BG	Total bases
	Type	Armour	Quality	Shooting	Impact	Melee			
Core Troops									
Devoted male worshippers	Warriors	Unarmoured	Average	–	Heavy Weapon	Heavy Weapon	5	10–12	30–120
	Mob	Unarmoured	Average	–	–	–	4	10–12	
Well-armed devoted male worshippers	Warriors	Unarmoured	Average	Musket*	–	–	6	6	12–24
	Light Foot	Unarmoured	Average	Musket	–	–	7	6	0–12
Infirm, women and children	Mob	Unarmoured	Poor	–	–	–	2	10–12	20–48
Optional Troops									
Fanatical followers	Warriors	Unarmoured	Superior	–	Heavy Weapon	Heavy Weapon	8	8–12	0–16
Cavalry	Horse	Unarmoured	Average	–	Pistol	Swordsmen	8	4	0–12 / 0–24
	Horse	Unarmoured	Poor	–	Pistol	Swordsmen	6	4	0–24 /

MONMOUTH REBELLION

This list covers the army raised by the Duke of Monmouth in the West Country in 1685, following the death of Charles II and the accession of James II. His rebellion ended with defeat at the Battle of Sedgemoor, near Bridgewater in Somerset, on 6 July.

James Scott, 1st Duke of Monmouth, was the illegitimate son of Charles II and as such had no legal entitlement to the throne. His uncle James, however, was very unpopular owing to his Catholic religion. The Protestant Monmouth hoped that a rebellion would attract vast popular support to his cause, allowing him to depose his uncle and claim the British throne for himself.

Monmouth intended to land in the West Country, where he believed the population were particularly supportive of his objectives. It was also planned that a simultaneous landing, led by the exiled Earl of Argyll, would take place in Scotland. Unfortunately, however, Argyll landed in Scotland first and, having bungled his efforts, was promptly arrested. Shortly thereafter, Argyll was beheaded on the same Maiden (early guillotine) which had seen off his father several years earlier.

Unaware of this significant setback to his plans, Monmouth landed at Lyme Regis on 11 June accompanied by less than one hundred officers and men. Significantly, however, he had brought large stores of armour and weapons with which to equip his potential new recruits. While the King's forces gathered to oppose the landing, Monmouth did have time to raise an army estimated as numbering anywhere between 3,500 and 7,000 men. Some of these were reasonably well-equipped and given training in the manoeuvres of the day, others were armed only with improvised weapons such as scythes etc.

The core of Monmouth's army, however, despite the short time available, was fairly well-trained, mainly due to the efforts of the professional soldiers he had brought with him.

Advancing, Monmouth had some initial success against local militias, and indeed reached the outskirts of Bath and Bristol before hearing of the approach of the King's main army. He then decided to retreat to Bridgewater and consider his options. He was deeply concerned about the ability of his newly raised forces to face a better trained and disciplined enemy, particularly in the open terrain of the West Country.

During the afternoon of 5 July, Monmouth viewed the Royal encampment from a church tower and conceived the idea of a night attack, which would give him the element of surprise, and also deprive the Royalist army of many of the advantages it would gain in a traditional battle. After dark, the rebels set forth, and were lucky to be missed by the Royalist army cavalry scouts. Nevertheless, their approach was detected and the Royal camp awakened. Some surprise was still possible, but Monmouth's men suddenly found their approach blocked by a substantial water obstacle over which they failed to find a crossing point. The battle then broke out, although this was really only an exchange of musketry across the water. The rebels gave a good account of themselves until they were outflanked by the Royalist horse. Under this pressure the rebels fell back, and this retreat degenerated into a rout.

Monmouth fled the field and, despite changing clothing with a peasant, was discovered the next day and arrested. Taken to London, he begged for his life at the feet of his uncle, the King. James was not in a forgiving mood and had him executed in

*Troopers of the Regiments of Horse, Sedgemoor, 1685, by Gerry Embleton © Osprey Publishing Ltd.
Taken from Men-at-Arms 267:* The British Army 1660–1704.

what must have been one of the most botched beheadings in history. It is said that after three strokes of the axe the executioner used a knife to finish the job.

Monmouth's followers fared little better in the aftermath, with many being executed while others were deported.

TROOP NOTES

Despite being considered by many as a yokel or peasant army, it is now accepted that the vast majority of the army was recruited from the middle classes and equally from men who were highly motivated and knew what they were fighting for.

Monmouth's army seems to have been fairly well-trained, but some shortage of muskets was evident, justifying classification as Musket*.

Other less well-trained and -armed foot did have to use scythes and other farm implements, although these men appear to have been kept in reserve. Interestingly, these troops seem to have been particularly feared by their opponents.

The cavalry wore armour and had weaponry equal to their foes. Their leader, however, seems to have been particularly ineffectual, and classification of some of the troops as "Poor" could be justified as a means of reflecting this.

The artillery was very gallant and joined the infantry in the close range fight across the water. When the army retreated, the guns covered the retreat and continued to give good service until isolated and destroyed by the Royalist cavalry.

As this is a small army, it might be more appropriate to consider battle groups as companies or troops rather than regiments.

Sedgemoor, 1685, by Stephen Walsh © Osprey Publishing Ltd. Taken from Warrior 43: Matchlock Musketeer.

MONMOUTH REBELLION

MONMOUTH REBELLION STARTER ARMY		
Commander-in-Chief	1	Field Commander
Sub-Commanders	2	2 x Troop Commander
Cavalry	2 BGs	Each comprising 4 bases of Cavalry: Average, Armoured Determined Horse – Impact Pistol, Melee Pistol
Cavalry	1 BG	4 bases of Cavalry: Poor, Armoured Determined Horse – Impact Pistol, Melee Pistol
Trained Foot	5 BGs	Each comprising 6 bases of Trained foot: 4 bases of Average, Unarmoured Medium Foot – Musket*; and 2 bases of Average, Unarmoured Heavy Foot – Pike
Untrained foot	1 BG	6 bases of Untrained foot: Average, Unarmoured Medium Foot – Heavy Weapon
Untrained foot	4 BGs	Each comprising 6 bases of Untrained foot: Poor, Unarmoured Medium Foot – Heavy Weapon
Artillery	1 BG	2 bases of Artillery – Average Light Artillery
Camp	1	Unfortified camp
Total	14 BGs	Camp, 12 mounted bases, 62 foot bases, 3 commanders

BUILDING A CUSTOMISED LIST USING OUR ARMY POINTS

Choose an army based on the maxima and minima in the list below. The following special instructions apply to this army:

- Commanders should be depicted as cavalry.
- There must be at least as many battle groups of Untrained foot fielded as Trained foot.

MONMOUTH REBELLION									
Territory Types: Agricultural									
C-in-C	Field Commander/Troop Commander						50/35	1	
Sub-commanders	Field Commander						50	0–2	
	Troop Commander						35	0–3	
Troop name	Troop Type			Capabilities			Points per base	Bases per BG	Total bases
	Type	Armour	Quality	Shooting	Impact	Melee			
Core Troops									
Trained foot	Medium Foot	Unarmoured	Average	Musket*	–	–	7	4	6	12–84
	Heavy Foot	Unarmoured	Average	–	Pike	Pike	5	2	
Untrained foot	Warriors	Unarmoured	Average	–	Heavy Weapon	Heavy Weapon	5	6	12–84
			Poor				3		
Cavalry	Determined Horse	Armoured	Average	–	Pistol	Pistol	15	4	4–12
			Poor				11		
Optional Troops									
Artillery	Light Artillery	–	Average	Light Artillery	–	–	12	2, 3 or 4	0–4

LATER LOUIS XIV FRENCH

*F*ollowing *the Peace of the Pyrenees* in 1659, and the death of his First Minister, Cardinal Mazarin, in 1661, the young Louis XIV assumed personal control of the government of France. Although bellicose by nature, and desperate for *gloire*, Louis appreciated that France was as yet in no condition to once again go to war, and that he would have to exercise patience before he could fulfil his dream of military glory. To ensure that France was once again in a position to wage war to further his ambitions, Louis undertook a number of reforms and appointed a series of capable men such as Colbert, Le Tellier and Louvois to high office. In a break with tradition, Louis did not give these offices to members of the old nobility, but to "new men", who were wholly dependent on the King.

Louis managed to wait until 1667 before commencing his wars. The pretext for his first war, subsequently known as The War of Devolution, was that as Spain had not paid the massive dowry due on his marriage to the Spanish infanta, Marie Thérèse, a condition of which was that she renounced her inheritance rights as the daughter of Philip IV of Spain, he was entitled to that inheritance on the death of Philip, which occurred in 1665. Louis decided that the Spanish possessions in the Low Countries would be an ideal restitution, and would aid France by securing part of her northern frontier. In 1667, led by Marshal Turenne, the French invaded Flanders and, in what was something of a procession, took fortress after fortress with little opposition. Unfortunately, this so alarmed the Dutch that they formed an alliance with England and Sweden to oppose Louis. Faced with a large scale war, Louis compromised and withdrew from Flanders, retaining only twelve of the fortified places he had taken. Turenne thought this a mistake, as he felt he could have finished the conquest in the next year.

French Line Infantry

LATER LOUIS XIV FRENCH

Following the War of Devolution, Louis felt betrayed by the Dutch, who, he had assumed, would not have been too concerned with the removal of the Spanish, against whom they had fought a long war of independence, and their replacement by a friendly power, to whit France. As a result, his next war would be directed against the Dutch, and has become known, unsurprisingly, as the Franco-Dutch War.

As with his first war, all initially went well for Louis as his armies, again led by Turenne assisted by the great Condé and the future Marshal Luxembourg, captured a whole series of fortresses, over-running large parts of the United Provinces. The Dutch, unable to face the French armies in the field, were forced to open the sluices and flood their land. It is worth noting that it was at the siege of Maastricht that Vauban first used the

Pikeman of the Régiment Douglas, and Musketeers of the Régiments Furstenberg and Lyonnais, 1666–69, by Francis Back © Osprey Publishing Ltd. Taken from Men-at-Arms 203: Louis XIV's Army.

system of parallels to approach the fortress, which thereafter became the norm in siege warfare. It was also where the real d'Artagnan was killed. Despite initial success, the war then followed the pattern of the War of Devolution, with an alliance formed against Louis to force him to withdraw. This led, in 1674, to the Battle of Seneffe, where Condé once again showed both his personal bravery, leading charges despite being so gout ridden he could not wear his boots, and his cavalier disregard for casualties. The casualty rate was higher than in any of Louis' wars until the War of the Spanish Succession, when armies were much larger.

The war also expanded into Germany, where Turenne and the great Imperialist general Montecuccoli engaged in the greatest war of manoeuvre of the age, punctuated by relatively indecisive battles which failed to knock either army out of the war. Alas for Louis, in 1675, whilst reconnoitring, Turenne was hit and killed by a speculative cannon shot from the Imperial lines. Montecuccoli commented "Today died a man who did honour to mankind". This brought the French campaign to a grinding halt. Later that year Condé retired, his ailments finally getting the better of him. The only positive for Louis was that Montecuccoli also retired, thus removing a talented opponent. The war expanded to include fighting in north Spain and Sicily, but the Low Countries and the Rhineland remained the major theatres of operations. The war ended in 1678 as Louis came to terms with his enemies. Although he had to give up his Dutch conquests, he obtained substantial territories from the Spanish as part of the settlement. One of the lasting effects of this war was that the Dutch Stadtholder, William III of Orange, became an inveterate enemy of Louis.

Despite the territory gained in the Franco-Dutch War, Louis was not yet satisfied that he had obtained all the lands France needed to be secure. He therefore engaged in a series of at best legally dubious "land grabs", based on some of the vaguer parts of the Treaty of Westphalia. These were mostly at the expense of the Spanish and Rhineland states. There was some fighting, and this is known as the War of the Reunions.

In 1685 Louis revoked his grandfather Henri IV's Edict of Nantes, which had given the Protestant Huguenots freedom of worship and a degree of political independence, both of which were unacceptable to the absolutist Louis. Although the revocation re-established Catholicism as the only legitimate religion in France, it caused up to half a million Huguenots to flee France and take up residence in countries that were opposed to Louis, such as England and the Dutch Republic. These refugees would, thereafter, work in opposition to France, and proved to be a ready source of recruits for the armies of Louis' enemies. Additionally, the refugees were amongst some of the most skilled and hard working in France, and again Louis suffered by their loss. The remaining Protestants were now persecuted in an attempt to force them to convert. Part of this involved the billeting of dragoons on Protestants, which led to the measures becoming known as Dragonnades.

Louis' last, and longest, war of the 17th century started in 1688, and is known by a variety of names – The War of the League of Augsburg after the coalition who opposed him, the Nine Years' War after its length, and the War of the Grand Alliance, again referring to his opponents, are the most common. It has also been described as Louis' "great miscalculation" by one modern authority. The war saw France faced by an alliance of England and the United Provinces (known as the Maritime Powers), Sweden, Spain, Austria, Savoy and a number of German states. The cause of the war was a dispute

LATER LOUIS XIV FRENCH

Musketeer of the Régiment des Gardes Françaises, Cavalryman of the Garde du Corps, and Grenadier à Cheval, 1675–80, by Francis Back © Osprey Publishing Ltd. Taken from Men-at-Arms 203: Louis XIV's Army.

over the succession to the archbishopric of Cologne, in which Louis had intervened to try to get a candidate acceptable to France elected. Once again the main theatre of war was the Low Countries and the Rhineland, with associated theatres in Savoy and Catalonia. Despite the length of the war, there were very few major land battles, Walcourt and Steenkirk being the most significant, and both French victories, although neither actually had much influence on the course of the war. Manoeuvre and, most importantly, sieges were the major features of this war. One reason for this may have been the indifferent quality of the generals on both sides. Certainly Louis had nobody of the ability and drive of a Turenne or Condé to call on. Marshal Luxembourg came close, but was probably held back by Louis' insistence on directing the war, which curtailed his freedom of action. The war was ruinously expensive for France – at one stage she had, on paper, over 400,000 men under arms, the highest number until the Revolutionary Wars a century later. The war ended with the Treaty of Ryswick, which left France with more or less what she had started with.

This list covers French armies from 1661 until the end of this period in 1698.

TROOP NOTES

At the start of the period covered by this list, French infantry companies comprised 60 musketeers and 40 pikemen, an organisation that had been set down by royal order in 1653. In February 1670 a new royal order reduced the numbers to 50 musketeers and 20 pikemen in a smaller company of 70 men. In practice, however, the number of pikemen was lower than theoretically required, and pikemen were recorded as discarding their pike to pick up and use the muskets of their fallen comrades. In 1692 Louis XIV recognised this fact and officially reduced the number of pikemen to 10 per company.

Guard infantry regiments appear to have retained their armour until the end of this period.

The bayonet, a French invention, was adopted early in this period.

French cavalry were recognised as possibly the best in Europe by this date, but at the start of the period covered by this list they were, in general, somewhat ill-disciplined, and thus we rate them

Gardes Suisses

as Cavaliers. From about 1670, with Turenne as Colonel-Général of Cavalry, discipline was much improved, and we change their classification to Determined Horse.

From 1679, two cavalrymen per company were given rifled carbines and called *carabiniers*. These were later expanded into a full company per regiment, and then, in 1693, all these companies were grouped together into the Royal Carabiniers. Although they carried a rifled carbine, in action they appear to have fought as other cavalry.

The Grenadiers à cheval de la Garde were formed in December 1676, being recruited from those infantry grenadiers considered the most brave in the army. Equipped with pistols, curved sabres, carbines and grenades, they were required to wear large moustaches to make them look even more striking and fearsome. They would spearhead the Maison du Roi in action, and at the Battle of Leuze in 1690 captured 5 enemy colours on their own.

LATER LOUIS XIV FRENCH STARTER ARMY (FROM 1691)		
Commander-in-Chief	1	Field Commander
Sub-Commanders	2	2 x Troop Commander
Guard led by Grenadiers a cheval	1 BG	2 bases of Guard led by Grenadiers a cheval: Elite, Unarmoured Determined Horse – Impact Pistol, Melee Pistol
Line cavalry	2 BGs	Each comprising 4 bases of Line cavalry: Superior, Unarmoured Determined Horse – Impact Pistol, Melee Pistol
Line cavalry	1 BG	4 bases of Line cavalry: Average, Unarmoured Determined Horse – Impact Pistol, Melee Pistol
Line infantry	3 BGs	Each comprising 6 bases of Line infantry: 5 bases of Average, Unarmoured Medium Foot – Musket*, Impact Foot, Bayonet; and 1 base of Average, Unarmoured Heavy Foot – Pike
Fusiliers du Roi	1 BG	4 bases of Fusiliers du Roi: Average, Unarmoured Medium Foot – Musket, Bayonet
Dragoons	1 BG	4 bases of Dragoons: Average, Unarmoured Dragoons – Musket
Artillery	1 BG	2 bases of Artillery – Average Medium Artillery
Camp	1	Unfortified camp
Total	10 BGs	Camp, 14 mounted bases, 28 foot bases, 3 commanders

BUILDING A CUSTOMISED LIST USING OUR ARMY POINTS

Choose an army based on the maxima and minima in the list below. The following special instructions apply to this army:

• Commanders should be depicted as guard cavalry.

• The army can only include one battle group of Guard led by Grenadiers a cheval.
• The army can only include one battle group of Hussars.
• If Catalan miquelets are used, no guard battle groups can be fielded and the army counts as "In Spain".
• The minimum marked * is reduced to 4 in Spain.

71

LATER LOUIS XIV FRENCH

Territory Types: Agricultural, Woodland, Hilly

C-in-C	Great Commander/Field Commander/Troop Commander						80/50/35	1	
Sub-commanders	Field Commander						50	0–2	
	Troop Commander						35	0–3	

Troop name		Troop Type			Capabilities			Points per base	Bases per BG	Total bases
		Type	Armour	Quality	Shooting	Impact	Melee			
Core Troops										
Guard cavalry of the Maison du Roi		Determined Horse	Unarmoured	Superior	–	Pistol	Pistol	18	4	0–8 (0–8)
Guard led by Grenadiers a cheval	Only from 1677	Determined Horse	Unarmoured	Elite	–	Pistol	Pistol	21	2–4	0–4
Line cavalry	Only before 1670	Cavaliers	Armoured / Unarmoured	Superior	–	Impact Mounted	Swordsmen	21 / 18	4	8–32 (*8–32)
	Only from 1670 to 1690	Determined Horse	Unarmoured	Superior	–	Impact Mounted	Swordsmen	20	4	
	Only from 1691	Determined Horse	Unarmoured	Superior	–	Pistol	Pistol	18	4	
	Only before 1670	Cavaliers	Armoured / Unarmoured	Average	–	Impact Mounted	Swordsmen	16 / 13	4	0–12
	Only from 1670 to 1690	Determined Horse	Unarmoured	Average	–	Impact Mounted	Swordsmen	14	4	
	Only from 1691	Determined Horse	Unarmoured	Average	–	Pistol	Pistol	12	4	
Carabiniers	Only from 1693	Horse	Unarmoured	Superior / Average	Carbine	–	Pistol	12 / 9	4	0–4
Guard infantry	Only before 1670	Medium Foot	Unarmoured	Superior	Musket*	Impact Foot + Bayonet	Bayonet	11	4	6 (0–18)
		Heavy Foot	Armoured	Superior	–	Pike	Pike	9	2	
	Only from 1670	Medium Foot	Unarmoured	Superior	Musket*	Impact Foot + Bayonet	Bayonet	11	5	6
		Heavy Foot	Armoured	Superior	–	Pike	Pike	9	1	
Line infantry	Only before 1670	Medium Foot	Unarmoured	Average	Musket*	Impact Foot + Bayonet	Bayonet	8	4	6 / 12–60
		Heavy Foot	Armoured	Average	–	Pike	Pike	6	2	
	Only before 1670	Medium Foot	Unarmoured	Average	Musket*	Impact Foot + Bayonet	Bayonet	8	4	6 / 0–30
		Heavy Foot	Unarmoured	Average	–	Pike	Pike	5	2	12–60
	Only from 1670 to 1690	Medium Foot	Unarmoured	Average	Musket*	Impact Foot + Bayonet	Bayonet	8	5	6 / 12–60
		Heavy Foot	Armoured	Average	–	Pike	Pike	6	1	
	Only from 1670	Medium Foot	Unarmoured	Average	Musket*	Impact Foot + Bayonet	Bayonet	8	5	6 / 12–60
		Heavy Foot	Unarmoured	Average	–	Pike	Pike	5	1	
Dragoons	Only before 1670	Dragoons	Unarmoured	Average	Musket	–	–	8	3–4	0–4
	Only from 1670									4–16
Artillery		Heavy Artillery	–	Average	Heavy Artillery	–	–	25	2,3 or 4	
		Medium Artillery	–	Average	Medium Artillery	–	–	20	2,3 or 4	2–4
		Light Artillery	–	Average	Light Artillery	–	–	12	2,3 or 4	

LATER LOUIS XIV FRENCH

Optional Troops											
Militia or newly raised regiments	Only before 1670	Medium Foot	Unarmoured	Poor	Musket*	Impact Foot + Bayonet	Bayonet	6	4	6	18–48 in Spain, 0–24 elsewhere
		Heavy Foot	Unarmoured	Poor	–	Pike	Pike	3	2		
	Only from 1670	Medium Foot	Unarmoured	Poor	Musket*	Impact Foot + Bayonet	Bayonet	6	5	6	
		Heavy Foot	Unarmoured	Poor	–	Pike	Pike	3	1		
Hussars	Only from 1692	Light Horse	Unarmoured	Average	Carbine	–	Swordsmen	9	2–4		0–4
Fusiliers du Roi	Only from 1671	Medium Foot	Unarmoured	Average	Musket	Bayonet	Bayonet	9	4–6		0–6
Catalan miquelets	Only in Spain	Light Foot	Unarmoured	Average	Musket	–	–	7	6–8		0–12
Allies											
English allies (Only from 1672 to 1674) – Restoration British											

Dragoons of Louis XIV's Army, 1680–98, by Francis Back © Osprey Publishing Ltd.

Taken from Men-at-Arms 203: Louis XIV's Army.

LATER LOUIS XIV FRENCH ALLIES									
Allied commander		Field Commander/Troop Commander						40/25	1
Troop name		**Troop Type**			**Capabilities**			Points per base	Bases per BG	Total bases
		Type	Armour	Quality	Shooting	Impact	Melee			
Line cavalry	Only before 1670	Cavaliers	Armoured	Superior	–	Impact Mounted	Swordsmen	21	4	0–12	4–12
			Unarmoured					18			
	Only from 1670 to 1690	Determined Horse	Unarmoured	Superior	–	Impact Mounted	Swordsmen	20	4		
	Only from 1691	Determined Horse	Unarmoured	Superior	–	Pistol	Pistol	18	4		
	Only before 1670	Cavaliers	Armoured	Average	–	Impact Mounted	Swordsmen	16	4	0–12	
			Unarmoured					13			
	Only from 1670 to 1690	Determined Horse	Unarmoured	Average	–	Impact Mounted	Swordsmen	14	4		
	Only from 1691	Determined Horse	Unarmoured	Average	–	Pistol	Pistol	12	4		
Guard infantry	Only before 1670	Medium Foot	Unarmoured	Superior	Musket*	Impact Foot + Bayonet	Bayonet	11	4	6	0–6
		Heavy Foot	Armoured	Superior		Pike	Pike	9	2		
	Only from 1670	Medium Foot	Unarmoured	Superior	Musket*	Impact Foot + Bayonet	Bayonet	11	5	6	
		Heavy Foot	Armoured	Superior	–	Pike	Pike	9	1		
Line infantry	Only before 1670	Medium Foot	Unarmoured	Average	Musket*	Impact Foot + Bayonet	Bayonet	8	4	6	6–24
		Heavy Foot	Armoured	Average	–	Pike	Pike	6	2		
		Medium Foot	Unarmoured	Average	Musket*	Impact Foot + Bayonet	Bayonet	8	4	6	
		Heavy Foot	Unarmoured	Average	–	Pike	Pike	5	2		
	Only from 1670 to 1690	Medium Foot	Unarmoured	Average	Musket*	Impact Foot + Bayonet	Bayonet	8	5	6	
		Heavy Foot	Armoured	Average	–	Pike	Pike	6	1		
	Only from 1670	Medium Foot	Unarmoured	Average	Musket*	Impact Foot + Bayonet	Bayonet	8	5	6	
		Heavy Foot	Unarmoured	Average	–	Pike	Pike	5	1		
Dragoons	Only from 1670	Dragoons	Unarmoured	Average	Musket	–	–	8	3–4	0–6	
Artillery		Medium Artillery	–	Average	Medium Artillery	–	–	20	2	0–2	
		Light Artillery	–	Average	Light Artillery	–	–	12	2		

HUNGARIAN KURUC REBELLION

*I*n 1671 Austria attempted to replace the existing Hungarian constitution, in the parts of Hungary it controlled, with a more absolutist system in line with that of Austria. As a result, from 1672 onwards there were a series of rebellions against the Austrians, the rebels being known as *kuruczok* (singular: *kuruc*). The government forces and their supporters, at least after 1678, were termed "*labanc*" (from the Hungarian word for "long hair", after the wigs worn by Austrian soldiers). Although initially a guerrilla movement, the *kuruc* movement attracted foreign support, including that of Louis XIV, who wished the Austrian Emperor to be distracted from Western Europe by problems in his own back-yard. The rebels also found an effective leader in Count Imre Thököly, and soon made significant progress.

In the early 1680s, as they prepared to go to war with Austria again, the Turks

Hungarian Officer

started to send military aid to the rebels, in the hope that this would divert and weaken the Austrians before the main invasion of 1683. Hungarian rebels acted in concert with the invading army, and some were present at the siege of Vienna. In the aftermath of the Turkish defeat, and the Austrian advance into Turkish Hungary, the rebels came to an accommodation with the Austrians, who tempered their demands for change in the constitution. By 1685 the major military activity of the rebellion was over. Despite this, some bands still acted in the Turkish interest, and in conjunction with Turkish armies, whilst others acted with the Austrians as they wished to back the winning side.

This list covers the Hungarian *kuruc* rebel armies fighting the Austrians from 1672 to 1685.

TROOP NOTES

The vast majority of the troops in the rebellious armies were traditional hussars, supplemented by a smaller number of armoured troops. Infantry were sometimes present, and were of the traditional haiduk variety.

HUNGARIAN KURUC REBELLION STARTER ARMY		
Commander-in-Chief	1	Field Commander
Sub-Commanders	2	2 x Troop Commander
Armoured hussars	1 BG	4 bases of Armoured hussars: Superior, Armoured Cavaliers – Light Lancers, Melee Pistol
Veteran hussars	1 BG	4 bases of Veteran hussars: Superior, Armoured Cavalry – Carbine, Melee Pistol
Hussars	2 BGs	Each comprising 4 bases of Hussars: Unarmoured, Average Cavalry – Carbine, Melee Pistol
Hussars	2 BGs	Each comprising 4 bases of Hussars: Unarmoured, Average Light Horse – Carbine, Melee Pistol
Haiduks or similar foot	1 BG	6 bases of Haiduks or similar foot: Average, Unarmoured Light Foot – Musket
Haiduks or similar foot	2 BGs	Each comprising 6 bases of Haiduks or similar foot: Average, Unarmoured Medium Foot – Musket, Swordsmen
Dragoons	2 BGs	Each comprising 3 bases of Dragoons: Average, Unarmoured Dragoons – Musket
Camp	1	Unfortified camp
Total	11 BGs	Camp, 24 mounted bases, 24 foot bases, 3 commanders

BUILDING A CUSTOMISED LIST USING OUR ARMY POINTS

Choose an army based on the maxima and minima in the list below. The following special instructions apply to this army:

• Commanders should be depicted as armoured or veteran hussars.

HUNGARIAN KURUC REBELLION									
Territory Types: Agricultural, Hilly, Woodlands									
C-in-C	Great Commander/Field Commander/Troop Commander						80/50/35	1	
Sub-commanders	Field Commander						50	0–2	
	Troop Commander						35	0–3	
Troop name	Troop Type			Capabilities			Points per base	Bases per BG	Total bases
	Type	Armour	Quality	Shooting	Impact	Melee			
Core Troops									
Armoured hussars	Cavaliers	Armoured	Superior	–	Light Lancers	Pistol	19	4–6	0–12
Hussars	Cavalry	Unarmoured	Average	Carbine	–	Pistol	10	4–6	12–72
				Bow	–	Swordsmen	10		
	Light Horse	Unarmoured	Average	Bow	–	Swordsmen	9		
				Carbine	–	Pistol	9		
Veteran hussars	Cavalry	Unarmoured	Superior	Carbine	–	Pistol	13	4–6	0–12
				Bow	–	Swordsmen	13		
		Armoured	Superior	Carbine	–	Pistol	16		
				Bow	–	Swordsmen	16		
	Light Horse	Unarmoured	Superior	Carbine	–	Pistol	12		
				Bow	–	Swordsmen	12		
Optional Troops									
Dragoons	Dragoons	Unarmoured	Average	Musket	–	–	8	3 or 4	0–12
Haiduks or similar foot	Light Foot	Unarmoured	Average	Musket	–	–	7	6–8	0–18 0–48
	Medium Foot	Unarmoured	Average	Musket	–	Swordsmen	8	6–8	0–48
Peasants	Mob	Unarmoured	Poor	–	–	–	2	8–12	0–20
Field Guns	Medium Artillery	–	Average	Medium Artillery	–	–	20	2	0–2
Light Guns	Light Artillery	–	Average	Light Artillery	–	–	12	2	
Allies									
Polish allies (Only in 1677) – Later Polish and Lithuanian									
Turkish allies (Only from 1682) – Later Ottoman Turkish – see FOGR Companion 3: *Clash of Empires*									

HUNGARIAN KURUC REBELLION ALLIES								
Allied commander	Field Commander/Troop Commander					40/25	1	
Troop name	Troop Type			Capabilities			Points per base	Bases per BG	Total bases
	Type	Armour	Quality	Shooting	Impact	Melee			
Armoured hussars	Cavaliers	Armoured	Superior	–	Light Lancers	Pistol	19	4	0–4
Hussars	Cavalry	Unarmoured	Average	Carbine	–	Pistol	10	4–6	6–24
				Bow	–	Swordsmen	10		
	Light Horse	Unarmoured	Average	Bow	–	Swordsmen	9		
				Carbine	–	Pistol	9		
Veteran Hussars	Cavalry	Unarmoured	Superior	Carbine	–	Pistol	13	4	0–4
				Bow	–	Swordsmen	13		
		Armoured	Superior	Carbine	–	Pistol	16		
				Bow	–	Swordsmen	16		
	Light Horse	Unarmoured	Superior	Carbine	–	Pistol	12		
				Bow	–	Swordsmen	12		
Haiduks or similar foot	Light Foot	Unarmoured	Average	Musket	–	–	7	6	0–6	0–12
	Medium Foot	Unarmoured	Average	Musket	–	Swordsmen	8	6–8	0–16

WAR OF THE LEAGUE OF AUGSBURG ANGLO-DUTCH

This list covers Anglo-Dutch armies during the War of the League of Augsburg, including the armies in Ireland, from 1689 to 1697.

The accession of William of Orange to the British thrones in 1688 as William III (William II in Scotland), and his position as Stadtholder of Holland, Zeeland, Utrecht, Overijssel and Guelders in the Dutch Republic, meant that during the remainder of his life Britain and Holland were effectively in a union.

Dragoon Officer

Although at the start of his reign William was faced by a war with his bitter enemy Louis XIV, he was forced to initially deal with the deposed James II who, with French assistance, had landed in Ireland to try and reclaim his crowns. William initially gave the prosecution of the war to his talented French Huguenot general Schomberg, a refugee from Louis' anti-Protestant campaign, but in 1690 he himself crossed to Ireland to take charge. James and William met in battle near the village of Oldbridge at a fording place on the river Boyne, the river giving its name to the battle that followed. Although hard fought, with William coming out the victor, the battle was not decisive, and is probably most important because as a result James' nerve once again failed him, and he fled to France, leaving his supporters to fight on without him. With James out of the picture, William returned to England, leaving the army in the

Musketeer of Hasting's Regiment, Captain of the Earl of Angus' Regiment, and Pikemen of the Earl of Argyll's Regiment, 1689, by Gerry Embleton © Osprey Publishing Ltd. Taken from Men-at-Arms 118: The Jacobite Rebellions 1689–1745.

charge of the Dutch general Godert de Ginkell. In 1691 it met the Jacobite army, now commanded by the Frenchman, the Marquis de St Ruth, at the battle of Aughrim. This was again hard fought, with higher casualties than at the Boyne, and it is entirely possible that St Ruth would have won the battle had he not been decapitated by a cannon ball at a critical point. Aughrim proved decisive, and the war in Ireland ended soon after.

William also faced some opposition in Scotland, but this he deemed insufficiently serious to require his personal attendance. Despite the defeat of General Mackay at Killiekrankie in 1689, the rebellion was snuffed out following the Battle of Cromdale the following year.

With his position in his new kingdoms now secure, William could concentrate on the war against Louis, and send more British troops to the continent. The campaigns of the Anglo-Dutch forces, with their Spanish and German allies, mainly revolved around sieges and positional warfare relating to them. Despite the huge numbers of men committed, major battles were rare, and those that did take place did not prove to be decisive.

British Line Infantry

William himself commanded at a number of engagements, such as Steenkirk and Neerwinden, where on both occasions he was bested by Marshal Luxemburg, the best of Louis' generals, despite catching the Marshal at a disadvantage in the former battle. The war came to an end in 1697 with the Treaty of Ryswick, and the treaty can be seen as a success for William as Louis was forced to recognise him as the rightful king of England, Scotland and Ireland, and the arrival of Britain as a major power. The Dutch received important trade concessions, and a string of fortresses in the Spanish Netherlands to act as a barrier to future French offensives. One of the most significant developments arising from the war was the founding, in 1694, of the Bank of England to provide a loan for the British government to allow it to finance the war.

TROOP NOTES

William's army in Ireland was based heavily on Dutch and other foreign troops, as he was concerned that the British troops may have retained some feelings of loyalty to James II. Many British troops were sent to Holland, therefore, under John Churchill (who despite joining William retained contacts with Jacobites throughout his life) to serve in

the stead of the reliable Dutch troops brought to England. New English regiments were raised to supplement the Dutch, and whilst these would be, perforce, raw at the start of the campaigns, they would be loyal to the new regime.

In addition to the Dutch troops, William raised a number of regiments from Huguenot refugees from Louis XIV's France. Again, these were used as they were seen as more reliable than native British troops. It is possible that the infantry had the same "press on" attitude as did their compatriots in Louis' armies, and so we allow them the same classification in this list. Although they also served after the war in Ireland, we assume they operated in the same way as other British and Dutch foot as they became assimilated.

The largest of William's foreign contingents in Ireland were the Danes, who performed exceptionally well at the battle of the Boyne in 1690, blunting a possibly decisive Jacobite counter-attack despite being themselves in some disorder from crossing the river.

Armies on the continent were based around Dutch and British infantry and cavalry, the British now trusted following William's victory in Ireland. Significant German and Danish contingents supplemented the Anglo-Dutch core, and as they were integrated into the army they are not treated as allied contingents.

A muster list of 1691 shows a small number of Spanish cavalry in William's army. However, Spanish contingents are best represented as allies owing to the historical distrust between them and the Dutch, despite their common purpose in the War of the League of Augsburg.

Surprising as it may seem, a number of Swedish regiments were loaned to William for the duration of the war.

WAR OF THE LEAGUE OF AUGSBURG ANGLO-DUTCH STARTER ARMY		
Commander-in-Chief	1	Field Commander
Sub-Commanders	2	2 x Troop Commander
British and Dutch cavalry	1 BG	4 bases of British and Dutch cavalry: Average, Armoured Determined Horse – Impact Pistol, Melee Pistol
British and Dutch cavalry	3 BGs	Each comprising 4 bases of British and Dutch cavalry: Average, Unarmoured Determined Horse – Impact Pistol, Melee Pistol
British and Dutch guard infantry	1 BG	6 bases of British and Dutch guard infantry: 5 bases of Superior, Unarmoured Medium Foot – Musket, Bayonet; and 1 base of Superior, Unarmoured Heavy Foot – Pike; and Superior Regimental Guns
British and Dutch line infantry	1 BG	6 bases of British and Dutch line infantry: 5 bases of Average, Unarmoured Medium Foot – Musket, Bayonet; and 1 base of Average, Unarmoured Heavy Foot – Pike; and Average Regimental Guns
British and Dutch line infantry	1 BG	Each comprising 6 bases of British and Dutch line infantry: 5 bases of Average, Unarmoured Medium Foot – Musket, Bayonet; and 1 base of Average, Unarmoured Heavy Foot – Pike
British fusiliers	1 BG	4 bases of Fusiliers: Average, Unarmoured Medium Foot – Musket, Bayonet
British and Dutch dragoons	1 BG	3 bases of British and Dutch dragoons: Average, Unarmoured Dragoons – Musket
Artillery	1 BG	2 bases of Artillery – Average Medium Artillery
Camp	1	Unfortified camp
Total	10 BGs	Camp, 16 mounted bases, 27 foot bases, 3 commanders

BUILDING A CUSTOMISED LIST USING OUR ARMY POINTS

Choose an army based on the maxima and minima in the list below. The following special instructions apply to this army:

- Commanders should be depicted as British or Dutch cavalry.
- As usual, Regimental Guns must be the same quality as the battle group.
- The number of Superior Danish infantry bases cannot exceed the number of Average ones.

The Death of the Duke of Schomberg at the Battle of the Boyne, 1690, by Graham Turner © Osprey Publishing Ltd. Taken from Campaign 160: Battle of the Boyne 1690.

WAR OF THE LEAGUE OF AUGSBURG ANGLO–DUTCH

Territory Types: Agricultural, Woodlands, Hilly

C-in-C	Great Commander/Field Commander/Troop Commander					80/50/35		1
Sub-commanders	Field Commander					50		0–2
	Troop Commander					35		0–3

Troop name	Troop Type			Capabilities			Points per base	Bases per BG	Total bases
	Type	Armour	Quality	Shooting	Impact	Melee			
Core Troops									
British and Dutch cavalry	Determined Horse	Armoured	Average	–	Pistol	Pistol	15	4	4–16
		Unarmoured					12		
Poor quality Dutch cavalry	Determined Horse	Unarmoured	Poor	–	Pistol	Pistol	9	4	0–8
British and Dutch guard infantry	Medium Foot	Unarmoured	Superior	Musket	Bayonet	Bayonet	11	5	6	0–18
	Heavy Foot	Unarmoured	Superior	–	Pike	Pike	8	1	
British and Dutch line infantry	Medium Foot	Unarmoured	Average	Musket	Bayonet	Bayonet	8	5	6	12–60
	Heavy Foot	Unarmoured	Average	–	Pike	Pike	5	1	
3-pdr battalion guns	Regimental Guns	–	Superior	Regimental Guns	Regimental Guns	–	12	n/a	0–1 per British and Dutch guard or line infantry BG
			Average				9		
British and Dutch dragoons	Dragoons	Unarmoured	Average	Musket	–	–	8	3–4	3–8
Artillery	Medium Artillery	–	Average	Medium Artillery	–	–	20	2, 3 or 4	2–4
	Light Artillery	–	Average	Light Artillery	–	–	12	2, 3 or 4	
Optional Troops									
British and Dutch garrison infantry	Medium Foot	Unarmoured	Poor	Musket	Bayonet	Bayonet	6	5	6	0–24
	Heavy Foot	Unarmoured	Poor	–	Pike	Pike	3	1	
Danish infantry	Medium Foot	Unarmoured	Superior	Musket	Bayonet	Bayonet	12	6	0–6	0–12
	Medium Foot	Unarmoured	Average	Musket	Bayonet	Bayonet	9	6	0–12	
Danish, German or Spanish cavalry	Determined Horse	Unarmoured	Average	–	Pistol	Pistol	12	4	0–4
	Determined Horse	Unarmoured	Average	Carbine	–	Pistol	13	4	
German infantry	Medium Foot	Unarmoured	Average	Musket	Bayonet	Bayonet	9	6	0–24
Swedish infantry	Medium Foot	Unarmoured	Average	Salvo	Salvo + Bayonet	Bayonet	8	4	6	0–12
	Heavy Foot	Unarmoured	Average	–	Pike	Pike	5	2	
British fusiliers	Medium Foot	Unarmoured	Average	Musket	Bayonet	Bayonet	9	4	0–4
Allies									
Spanish allies – Later Spanish (Flanders options)									

WAR OF THE LEAGUE OF AUGSBURG ANGLO-DUTCH

Special Campaigns											
Only in Ireland 1689–1691											
German infantry, Swedish infantry and British fusiliers cannot be used. Double the usual number of Danish infantry can be used, and at least 2 BGs of them must be fielded.											
New British infantry regiments	Only in 1691	Medium Foot	Unarmoured	Average	Musket	–	–	8	5	6	6–24
		Heavy Foot	Unarmoured	Average	–	Pike	Pike	5	1		
	Any date	Medium Foot	Unarmoured	Poor	Musket	–	–	6	5	6	
		Heavy Foot	Unarmoured	Poor	–	Pike	Pike	3	1		
Huguenot infantry		Medium Foot	Unarmoured	Average	Musket*	Impact Foot + Bayonet	Bayonet	8	5	6	0–12
		Heavy Foot	Unarmoured	Average	–	Pike	Pike	5	1		
Huguenot cavalry		Determined Horse	Unarmoured	Superior		Pistol	Pistol	18	2		0–2

WAR OF THE LEAGUE OF AUGSBURG ANGLO-DUTCH ALLIES

Allied commander	Field Commander/Troop Commander						40/25		1	
Troop name	**Troop Type**			**Capabilities**			**Points per base**	**Bases per BG**	**Total bases**	
	Type	Armour	Quality	Shooting	Impact	Melee				
British and Dutch cavalry	Determined Horse	Armoured	Average	–	Pistol	Pistol	15	4	4–8	
		Unarmoured					12			
Poor quality Dutch cavalry	Determined Horse	Unarmoured	Poor	–	Pistol	Pistol	9	4	0–4	
British and Dutch guard infantry	Medium Foot	Unarmoured	Superior	Musket	Bayonet	Bayonet	11	5	6	0–6
	Heavy Foot	Unarmoured	Superior	–	Pikemen	Pikemen	8	1		
British and Dutch line infantry	Medium Foot	Unarmoured	Average	Musket	Bayonet	Bayonet	8	5	6	6–24
	Heavy Foot	Unarmoured	Average	–	Pikemen	Pikemen	5	1		
3-pdr battalion guns	Regimental Guns	–	Superior	Regimental Guns	Regimental Guns	–	12	n/a	0–1 per British and Dutch guard or line infantry BG	
			Average				9			
British and Dutch dragoons	Dragoons	Unarmoured	Average	Musket	–	–	8	2 or 3	0–3	
Artillery	Medium Artillery	–	Average	Medium Artillery	–	–	20	2	0–2	
	Light Artillery	–	Average	Light Artillery	–	–	12	2		

Musketeer and Pikeman of King William's Army, and Trooper of King James' Army, Ireland, 1691, by Gerry Embleton © Osprey Publishing Ltd. Taken from Men-at-Arms 267: The British Army 1660–1704.

JACOBITE IRISH

This list covers the Jacobite forces which fought in Ireland during the period 1689 to 1691, with a view to returning James II to the crowns of England, Scotland and Ireland.

Following the landing of William of Orange on English soil, James II's efforts to repel the invasion were dithery at best and, after a short period, he took the easy option and fled to France. This flight provided the English parliament with the opportunity to declare that he had abdicated and to proclaim William and Mary (who was James' daughter) as joint monarchs.

James had, however, far from conceded defeat, and petitioned the French King to support him in his efforts to regain the crowns of his three kingdoms. A rebellion in support of his cause had already broken out in Scotland, but Ireland provided an even more fertile ground for rebellion owing to the high proportion of Catholics, who could be relied on to support his cause. Anxious to deflect English attention away from continental wars, Louis XIV agreed to support James with some troops and ships, but his most important contribution would be the provision of arms and equipment. These were essential in any efforts to raise an Irish Catholic army.

Even before James' arrival in the country, Catholic supporters had risen in support of the exiled Stuart King and had some early successes, which boded well for the future. James' presence in Ireland was the signal required for more support, and it was with a substantial army at his back that he set off to capture the Protestant stronghold

Antrim Regiment Infantryman

of Derry. The omens for success were good, as up to this point William was more concerned with securing his position in England than with Ireland. It was with some confidence, therefore, that James called on Derry to surrender. Indeed it looked like this might be a formality, but at the last moment some of the Derry apprentice boys stiffened the resistance and fired on James' party, killing one of his aides. Frustrated, James settled down to a siege which seemed certain to be successful.

In England, however, William at last turned his eyes to Ireland and resolved to break the siege of Derry. One of his generals eventually forced a barricaded river, and supplies were brought into the town, effectively breaking the siege. James fell back to Dublin, where he received the news that William had also landed in Ireland and was moving south towards Dublin. Realising that a battle for Ireland was inevitable, James moved north to the River Boyne, which presented the best defensible position between William's army and Dublin. The two armies faced off for a day, but then James was informed that William was carrying out a flanking march with a view to crossing further downstream. James quickly mobilised about two thirds of his army (including his French regulars) and headed off to the west with a view to intercepting the march. He eventually intercepted William's force, but a large heavily overgrown gully lay between the two forces, making any combat impossible. Even worse news then reached James. William had in fact only sent a small proportion of his force on the flank march, while the remainder of his army was now attacking across the Boyne. Amazingly, James did nothing while his heavily outnumbered forces put up a gallant resistance against William's attack. Receiving word that his

King James' Army at the Gates of Derry, 1689, by Graham Turner © Osprey Publishing Ltd. Taken from Campaign 160: Battle of the Boyne 1690.

forces at the Boyne had been defeated, James then led the rest of the army back to Dublin, being the first man into the City and also the herald of disaster. Shortly thereafter, he fled back to France and left his followers to their fate.

Although dismayed by his cowardly flight, and indeed the removal of the French regulars, the Jacobites fought on. At the Battle of Aughrim in 1691, they nearly won a decisive victory, but the death of their commander and the superiority of the opposition in men, training and equipment turned the tide. Following this, the Jacobite cause slowly withered, although the bitterness between Protestant

Zurlauber Regiment.

and Catholic simmered on, creating the hotbed of violence that would be Irish history for the next three hundred years.

TROOP NOTES

Despite the common belief that the Irish Jacobites were poorly armed, they were in fact the recipients of significant arms shipments from the French King. This allowed the better equipped regiments to have a significant number of firearms. The best equipped had ratios of pike and musket similar to contemporary French units, but the majority were closer to the now old-fashioned 1:2 ratio, and a few had more pikes, and indeed half pikes, than this. Bayonets were in short supply.

The quality of the Irish foot was variable, hence the requirement for a proportion to be Poor.

JACOBITE IRISH

Patrick Sarsfield, first Earl of Lucan, although described by James II as "a brave fellow who had no head", was a particularly effective cavalry commander and his troops are given the option of classification as Cavaliers to reflect his gung ho style.

The French exchanged six of their regiments to replace six Irish regiments in an effort to bring some much needed stiffening to the Irish army. Unfortunately, some accounts describe the men in these regiments as being the dregs of the earth and indeed the ale houses. Thus an option to make some of them Poor is provided. As the Irish regiments which went to France formed the basis of the famous "Wild Geese", King Louis undoubtedly got the better of the bargain. The French regiments were withdrawn after the Boyne, so are not available after 1690.

James II was a particularly inept commander, and as such a rating as a troop commander is required. His reputation was further tarnished by the fact that after the Boyne he was in the forefront of the retreat and brought the first news of the debacle to Dublin.

He fled the country thereafter, and has the unenviable distinction of being hated by both sides, while to this day William of Orange is only hated by one side. He became known to the Irish as *Séamus an Chaca* (James the Turd).

In 1691 the Frenchman St Ruth was in command, and seemed a very competent as well as experienced commander. He was close to winning the Battle of Aughrim before being decapitated by a stray cannonball. Before this, Jacobite command was average at best.

The Raparees were bodies of irregular guerrillas who sniped at and generally harassed the Williamite forces from ambush. When the Williamite cavalry caught them in the open, however, they were generally either butchered in great numbers during the fight or summarily executed afterwards.

James II's Foot Guards

JACOBITE IRISH STARTER ARMY		
Commander-in-Chief	1	Field Commander
Sub-Commanders	2	2 x Troop Commander
Horse guards	1 BG	4 bases of Horse guards: Superior, Armoured Determined Horse – Impact Pistol, Melee Pistol
Horse guards	1 BG	4 bases of Horse guards: Average, Armoured Determined Horse – Impact Pistol, Melee Pistol
Other cavalry	1 BG	4 bases of Other cavalry: Average, Unarmoured Determined Horse – Impact Pistol, Melee Pistol
Foot guards	1 BG	6 bases of Foot guards: 5 bases of Superior, Unarmoured Medium Foot – Musket, Bayonet; and 1 base of Superior, Unarmoured Heavy Foot – Pike
Less well-equipped foot	2 BGs	Each comprising 6 bases of Less well equipped foot: 4 bases of Average, Unarmoured Medium Foot – Musket; and 2 bases of Average, Unarmoured Heavy Foot – Pike
Less well-equipped foot	2 BGs	Each comprising 6 bases of Less well equipped foot: 4 bases of Poor, Unarmoured Medium Foot – Musket; and 2 bases of Poor, Unarmoured Heavy Foot – Pike
Raparees	2 BGs	Each comprising 4 bases of Raparees: Unarmoured, Average Light Foot – Musket
Dragoons	1 BG	3 bases of Dragoons: Average, Unarmoured Dragoons – Musket
Camp	1	Unfortified camp
Total	11 BGs	Camp, 12 mounted bases, 41 foot bases, 3 commanders

BUILDING A CUSTOMISED LIST USING OUR ARMY POINTS

Choose an army based on the maxima and minima in the list below. The following special instructions apply to this army:

- Commanders should be depicted as horse guards.

- At least half the total number of battle groups of less well-equipped foot and badly equipped foot must be Poor quality.
- At least half the number of battle groups of Militia must be Poor quality.
- The C-in-C cannot be a Great Commander before 1691.
- If James is C-in-C he must be a Troop Commander.

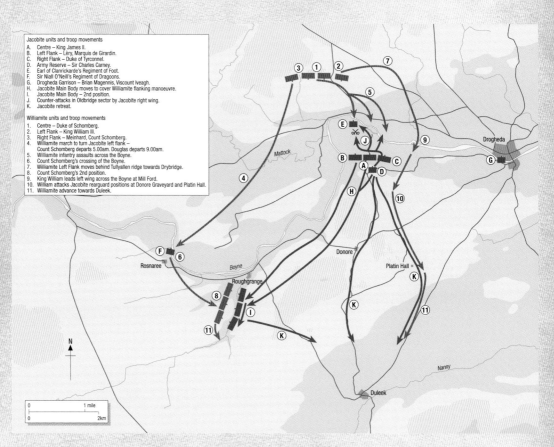

Jacobite units and troop movements

A. Centre – King James II.
B. Left Flank – Léry, Marquis de Girardin.
C. Right Flank – Duke of Tyrconnel.
D. Army Reserve – Sir Charles Carney.
E. Earl of Clanrickarde's Regiment of Foot.
F. Sir Niall O'Neill's Regiment of Dragoons.
G. Drogheda Garrison – Brian Magennis, Viscount Iveagh.
H. Jacobite Main Body moves to cover Williamite flanking manoeuvre.
I. Jacobite Main Body – 2nd position.
J. Counter-attacks in Oldbridge sector by Jacobite right wing.
K. Jacobite retreat.

Williamite units and troop movements

1. Centre – Duke of Schomberg.
2. Left Flank – King William III.
3. Right Flank – Meinhard, Count Schomberg.
4. Williamite march to turn Jacobite left flank – Count Schomberg departs 5.00am. Douglas departs 9.00am.
5. Williamite infantry assaults across the Boyne.
6. Count Schomberg's crossing of the Boyne.
7. Williamite Left Flank moves behind Tullyallen ridge towards Drybridge.
8. Count Schomberg's 2nd position.
9. King William leads left wing across the Boyne at Mill Ford.
10. William attacks Jacobite rearguard positions at Donore Graveyard and Platin Hall.
11. Williamite advance towards Duleek.

The Battle of the Boyne, 1 July 1690 © Osprey Publishing Ltd. Taken from Campaign 160: Battle of the Boyne 1690.

JACOBITE IRISH

Territory Types: Agricultural, Woodlands, Hilly

Troop name		Troop Type			Capabilities			Points per base	Bases per BG	Total bases
		Type	Armour	Quality	Shooting	Impact	Melee			
C-in-C		Great Commander/Field Commander/Troop Commander						80/50/35	1	
Sub-commanders		Field Commander						50	0–2	
		Troop Commander						35	0–3	
Core Troops										
Horse guards		Determined Horse	Armoured	Superior	–	Pistol	Pistol	21	4	0–4	4–8
		Cavaliers	Armoured	Superior	–	Pistol	Pistol	19		
		Determined Horse	Armoured	Average	–	Pistol	Pistol	15	4	4–8
Other cavalry		Determined Horse	Unarmoured	Average	–	Pistol	Pistol	12	4	4–12
Foot guards		Medium Foot	Unarmoured	Superior	Musket	Bayonet	Bayonet	11	5	6	0–6
		Heavy Foot	Unarmoured	Superior	–	Pike	Pike	8	1	
Veteran infantry		Medium Foot	Unarmoured	Average	Musket	Bayonet	Bayonet	8	5	6	0–12
		Heavy Foot	Unarmoured	Average	–	Pike	Pike	5	1	
Less well-equipped foot		Medium Foot	Unarmoured	Average	Musket	–	–	8	4	6	18–72
		Heavy Foot	Unarmoured	Average	–	Pike	Pike	5	2	
		Medium Foot	Unarmoured	Poor	Musket	–	–	6	4	6
		Heavy Foot	Unarmoured	Poor	–	Pike	Pike	3	2	
Dragoons		Dragoons	Unarmoured	Average	Musket	–	–	8	3 or 4	3–8
				Poor				6	
Artillery		Medium Artillery	–	Average	Medium Artillery	–	–	20	2, 3 or 4	0–4
Optional Troops										
Raparees		Light Foot	Unarmoured	Average	Musket	–	–	7	4–6	0–10
				Poor				5	
Badly equipped foot		Medium Foot	Unarmoured	Average	Musket*	–	–	7	4	6	0–24
		Heavy Foot	Unarmoured	Average	–	Pike	Pike	5	2	
		Medium Foot	Unarmoured	Poor	Musket*	–	–	5	4	6
		Heavy Foot	Unarmoured	Poor	–	Pike	Pike	3	2	
Militia		Warriors	Unarmoured	Average	–	Heavy Weapon	Heavy Weapon	5	6	0–24
				Poor				3	
French infantry	Only in 1690	Medium Foot	Unarmoured	Average	Musket*	Impact Foot + Bayonet	Bayonet	8	5	6	0–24
		Heavy Foot	Unarmoured	Average	–	Pike	Pike	5	1	
		Medium Foot	Unarmoured	Poor	Musket*	Impact Foot + Bayonet	Bayonet	6	5	6
		Heavy Foot	Unarmoured	Poor	–	Pike	Pike	3	1	

SCOTS JACOBITE REBELLION

This list covers the Scots Jacobite forces that fought in the rebellion of 1689–1690 which sought to return the deposed King James II to his throne.

When the news reached Scotland that King James had been deposed and replaced with William and Mary, the Scots, who at this time had an independent parliament, had to decide their own position. The main supporter of James was his old friend, the nemesis of the Covenanters, John Graham of Claverhouse (recently ennobled as Viscount Dundee). The supporters of King William, however, were better organised and more numerous, and it soon became clear to Dundee that he had no choice but to flee Edinburgh and hope to raise support for James elsewhere. With Dundee were only fifty men, the remnants of his old dragoon regiment.

Dundee had hoped to take Stirling, but dallied too long and had to fall back to his home area of Dundee. There, in front of an unenthusiastic citizenry, Dundee raised the Royal standard on

Highlanders

the Law Hill, before fleeing north again in search of an army.

In the North, the Catholic clans rallied to Dundee, who, like Montrose before him, had the ability to motivate and inspire these warlike Highlanders. Having raised around 2,000 men, he marched South, and on 27 July met the Government forces, some 3,500 strong under General Mackay of Scourie, at Killiekrankie.

Dundee, although heavily outnumbered, did hold the high ground, and also had knowledge of the fact that most of Mackay's troops were green and untried. Both sides seemed reluctant to take the initiative, but as the darkness closed in Dundee unleashed his Highlanders down the hill.

The government troops managed two volleys, allegedly killing and wounding 700 Jacobites – almost one third of the army – before the Highland avalanche hit their line. The government troops, badly deployed, with significant gaps in their line, and still attempting to fit their plug bayonets, disintegrated into a fleeing mob. The battle was won for the Jacobites.

The greatest loss, however, was the death of Dundee, who had ignored Lochiel's warning to stay out of the battle and spurred forward with his small body of horse. A musket ball travelled under his breastplate and brought him down. The breastplate still exists, with a neat hole in it – added later by a budding entrepreneur with an eye on the tourist industry.

With the death of Dundee, command fell on the Irishman Cannon, who lacked Dundee's ability to motivate the clansmen. Cannon led the Highlanders south to Dunkeld, which was held by a newly raised government regiment, fittingly consisting of ex-Covenanters. There, in a vicious

Highland Clansmen, 1689, by Gerry Embleton © Osprey Publishing Ltd. Taken from Men-at-Arms 118: The Jacobite Rebellions 1689–1745.

house-to-house battle totally unsuited to the Highland way of warfare, the Jacobites could make no progress, and eventually moved north again to lick their wounds. The inevitable break-up of the army took place as winter set in.

In the following year, the clans came out again under Major General Thomas Buchan. The army this time, however, was probably less than a thousand men. The endeavour did not last long, as a dawn attack by Government forces dispersed the Highland host at the Battle of Cromdale. The rebellion was over.

Interestingly, the Battle of Cromdale lives on in the famous Scottish ballad, "The Haughs O'Cromdale", albeit with a slightly different ending. The balladeer, obviously of Jacobite tendencies, recorded the events of the first day accurately. He then has the Highlanders rallied by Montrose (dead for some 30 years) and, during a second day's action, destroying the redcoats. These redcoats are also transformed into "Cromwell's men", allowing the ballad to finish with the refrain "of twenty thousand Cromwell's men a thousand fled to Aberdeen. The rest of them lie on the plain; they're on the Haughs of Cromdale."

TROOP NOTES

The armoured cavalry represent the remains of Dundee's own dragoon regiment, while the other less well-armed horse were a small body provided by the Earl of Dunfermline.

The make-up of the Irish contingent which joined Dundee is a bit of a mystery, but they certainly appear to have had pike and shot. The proportion of pike was likely to be higher than in the units of their English counterparts. In any case, it would appear that they just stormed down the slope with the Highlanders as part of the wild charge.

Certain clans performed better than others, so a degree of latitude has been allowed in rating.

The skirmishers represent a small body of musketeers detached by Cameron of Lochiel to occupy a small group of buildings at Killiekrankie, from where they fired on the Government line, making a nuisance of themselves.

SCOTS JACOBITE REBELLION STARTER ARMY		
Commander-in-Chief	1	Field Commander
Sub-Commanders	2	2 x Troop Commander
Dundee's dragoon remnants	1 BG	2 bases of Dundee's dragoon remnants: Superior, Armoured Determined Horse – Impact Pistol, Melee Pistol
Volunteer horse	1 BG	2 bases of Volunteer horse: Average, Unarmoured Determined Horse – Impact Pistol, Melee Pistol
Motivated and well-led Highlanders	2 BGs	Each comprising 6 bases of Motivated and well-led Highlanders: Superior, Unarmoured Warriors – Musket*, Impact Foot, Swordsmen
Highlanders	4 BGs	Each comprising 6 bases of Highlanders: Average, Unarmoured Warriors – Musket*, Impact Foot, Swordsmen
Irish	1 BG	6 bases of Irish: 4 bases of Average, Unarmoured Medium Foot – Musket; and 2 bases of Average Unarmoured Heavy Foot – Pike
Lochiel's skirmishers	1 BG	6 bases of Lochiel's skirmishers: Average, Unarmoured Light Foot – Musket, Swordsmen
Camp	1	Unfortified camp
Total	10 BGs	Camp, 4 mounted bases, 48 foot bases, 3 commanders

BUILDING A CUSTOMISED LIST USING OUR ARMY POINTS

Choose an army based on the maxima and minima in the list below. The following special instructions apply to this army:

- The commander-in-chief should be depicted as mounted and in lowland dress while sub commanders should be highland chiefs with their pipers and clan standard bearers.
- If dispirited Highlanders are used, no motivated and well-led Highlanders can be used.

SCOTS JACOBITE REBELLION

Territory Types: Agricultural, Woodland, Hilly

Troop name	Troop Type			Capabilities			Points per base	Bases per BG	Total bases
C-in-C	Great Commander/Field Commander/Troop Commander						80/50/35	1	
Sub-commanders	Field Commander						50	0–2	
	Troop Commander						35	0–3	
	Type	Armour	Quality	Shooting	Impact	Melee	Points per base	Bases per BG	Total bases
Core Troops									
Motivated and well-led Highlanders	Warriors	Unarmoured	Superior	Musket*	Impact Foot	Swordsmen	11	6–8	0–18
Highlanders	Warriors	Unarmoured	Average	Musket*	Impact Foot	Swordsmen	8	6–8	24–102
Dispirited Highlanders	Warriors	Unarmoured	Poor	Musket*	Impact Foot	Swordsmen	6	6–8	0–36
Optional Troops									
Dundee's dragoon remnants	Determined Horse	Armoured	Superior	–	Pistol	Pistol	21	2	0–2
Volunteer horse	Determined Horse	Unarmoured	Average	–	Pistol	Pistol	12	2	0–2
Lochiel's skirmishers	Light Foot	Unarmoured	Average	Musket	–	Swordsmen	8	6	0–6
Irish	Medium Foot	Unarmoured	Average	Musket	–	–	8	4	6	0–6
	Heavy Foot	Unarmoured	Average	–	Pike	Pike	5	2	

APPENDIX 1 – USING THE LISTS

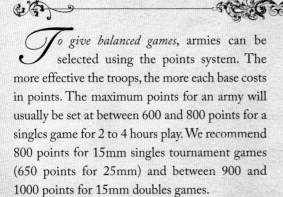

To give balanced games, armies can be selected using the points system. The more effective the troops, the more each base costs in points. The maximum points for an army will usually be set at between 600 and 800 points for a singles game for 2 to 4 hours play. We recommend 800 points for 15mm singles tournament games (650 points for 25mm) and between 900 and 1000 points for 15mm doubles games.

The army lists specify which troops can be used in a particular army. No other troops can be used. The number of bases of each type in the army must conform to the specified minima and maxima. Troops that have restrictions on when they can be used cannot be used with troops with a conflicting restriction. For example, troops that can only be used "before 1676" cannot be used with troops that can only be used "from 1676".

All special instructions applying to an army list must be adhered to. They also apply to allied contingents supplied by the army.

All armies must have a C-in-C and at least one other commander. No army can have more than 4 commanders in total, including C-in-C, sub-commanders and allied commanders.

All armies must have a supply camp. This is free unless fortified. A fortified camp can only be used if specified in the army list. Field fortifications and portable defences can only be used if specified in the army list.

Allied contingents can only be used if specified in the army list. Most allied contingents have their own allied contingent list, to which they must conform unless the main army's list specifies otherwise.

BATTLE GROUPS

All troops are organized into battle groups. Commanders, supply camps and field fortifications are not troops and are not assigned to battle groups. Portable defences are not troops, but are assigned to specific battle groups.

Battle groups must comply with the following restrictions:

- The number of bases in a battle group must correspond to the range specified in the list.
- Each battle group must initially comprise an even number of bases (not counting regimental gun markers), with the following exceptions. These can only be used if specified by the list:
  - A battle group can only initially have 3 bases if this is explicitly stated in the list: e.g. if the battle group size is specified in the form "2,3,4", and not if specified in the form "2-4".
- A battle group can only initially have 7 bases if it is specified in the list as a Swedish brigade formation.
- A battle group can only initially have 9 bases if this is explicitly stated in the list: e.g. if the battle group size is specified in the form "6,9,12", and not if specified in the form "6-12".
- A battle group can only include troops from one line in a list, unless the list specifies a mixed formation by indicating the battle group to be of types from more than one line: e.g. 2 pike and 4 shot – as specified in the list example below.
- All troops in a battle group must be of the same quality. Where a choice of quality is given in a list, this allows battle groups to differ from each other. It does not override the above rule for each battle group.
- All troops in a battle group with the same troop type and combat capabilities must be of the same armour class. Where a choice of armour class is given in a list, this allows battle groups to differ from each other. It does not override the above rule for each battle group.

EXAMPLE LIST

Here is a section of an actual army list, which will help us to explain the basics and some special features. The list specifies the following items for each historical type included in the army:

- Troop Type - comprising Type, Armour and Quality.

Polish Standard Bearer

- Capabilities – comprising Shooting, Impact and Melee capabilities.
- Points cost per base.
- Minimum and maximum number of bases in each battle group.
- Minimum and maximum number of bases in the army.

James II Foot Guards

Troop name		Troop Type			Capabilities			Points per base	Bases per BG	Total bases
		Type	Armour	Quality	Shooting	Impact	Melee			
Hussars		Determined Horse	Armoured	Superior	–	Impact Mounted	Swordsmen	23	4–6	4–16
Armoured Cossacks or pancerni	Only before 1676	Cavalry	Armoured	Superior	Carbine	–	Pistol	16	4–6	4–36
				Average				12		
	Only from 1676	Cavalry	Armoured	Superior	–	Light Lancers	Pistol	15	4–6	
				Average				11		
Lithuanian petyhortsy		Cavalry	Armoured	Average	Bow*	Light Lancers	Swordsmen	12	4–6	
			Unarmoured					10		
Other Cossacks		Cavalry	Unarmoured	Average	Carbine		Swordsmen	10	4–6	
		Cavalry	Unarmoured	Average	Bow		Swordsmen	10	4–6	
German "raytars" or arkebusiers	Only before 1650	Horse	Armoured	Average	–	Pistol	Pistol	10	4	4–12
				Poor				7		
		Horse	Unarmoured	Average	–	Pistol	Pistol	8	4	
				Poor				6		
	Only from 1640	Determined Horse	Armoured	Average	–	Pistol	Pistol	15	4	
				Poor				11		
		Determined Horse	Unarmoured	Average	–	Pistol	Pistol	12	4	
				Poor				9		
"German"-style infantry regiments	Only before 1680	Medium Foot	Unarmoured	Average	Musket	–	–	8	4	6
		Heavy Foot	Unarmoured	Average	–	Pike	Pike	5	2	
		Medium Foot	Unarmoured	Poor	Musket	–	–	6	4	6
		Heavy Foot	Unarmoured	Poor	–	Pike	Pike	3	2	6–48
Polish-style infantry regiments	Only from 1673	Medium Foot	Unarmoured	Average	Musket	Heavy Weapon	Heavy Weapon	8	6	
				Poor				6		
Light guns attached to infantry regiments	Only from 1652 to 1662	Regimental Guns	–	Average	Regimental Guns	Regimental Guns	–	9	n/a	0–1 per "German"-style infantry regiment
				Poor				7		
Artillery		Medium Artillery	–	Average	Medium Artillery	–	–	20	2	0–2 / 0–4
		Light Artillery	–	Average	Light Artillery	–	–	12	2, 3 or 4	0–4

Polish Dragoons

In addition, the special instructions to the list state the following:

- There must be at least as many Cossack, pancerni or petyhortsy battle groups fielded as there are hussar battle groups.
- From 1652 to 1662 there must be at least as many raytar bases as hussar bases.
- As usual, Regimental Guns must be the same quality as the battle group.

SPECIAL FEATURES:

- Hussars must be organized in battle groups of 4 or 6 bases. The army must include at least 4 bases of hussars, and cannot include more than 16.
- Armoured Cossacks or pancerni must be organized in battle groups of 4 or 6 bases. Their quality can be Superior or Average, but all the bases in each battle group must have the same quality grading. Different battle groups can have different quality gradings. Before 1676 their capabilities are Shooting Carbine, Melee Pistol. From 1676 their capabilities are Impact Light Lancers, Melee Pistol. These dates are mutually exclusive, so an army cannot include both types.
- Lithuanian petyhortsy must be organized in battle groups of 4 or 6 bases. Their armour

rating can be Armoured or Unarmoured, but all the bases in each battle group must have the same armour rating. Different battle groups can have different armour ratings.

- Other Cossacks must be organized in battle groups of 4 or 6 bases. Their capabilities can either be Shooting Carbine, Melee Swordsmen or Shooting Bow, Melee Swordsmen. All the bases in each battle group must have the same capabilities, but different battle groups can have different capabilities.
- The army must include at least 4 bases of Armoured Cossacks or pancerni, Lithuanian petyhortsy or other Cossacks, which can be of any one of these types. It cannot include more than 36 bases of all these types put together. In addition, the special instructions require that there must be at least as many Cossack, pancerni or petyhortsy battle groups fielded as there are hussar battle groups.
- German raytars or arkebusiers must be organized in battle groups of 4 bases. Before 1640 they must be rated as Horse. From 1650 they must be rated as Determined Horse. From 1640 to 1649 they can be rated either as Horse or Determined Horse. All the bases in each battle group must be rated the same, but different battle groups can be rated differently. Their armour rating can be Armoured or Unarmoured, but all the bases in each battle group must have the same armour rating. Different battle groups can have different armour ratings. Their quality can be Average or Poor, but all the bases in each battle group must have the same quality grading. Different battle groups can have different quality gradings. The army must include at least 4 bases of German raytars or arkebusiers, and cannot include more than 12. In addition, the special instructions require that from 1652 to

*Men of the Tangiers Garrison, 1669, by Gerry Embleton © Osprey Publishing Ltd.
Taken from Men-at-Arms 267:* The British Army 1660–1704.

1662 there must be at least as many raytar bases in the army as hussar bases.

- "German"-style infantry regiments can only be used before 1680. They must be organised in battle groups comprising 2 bases of pike and 4 bases of shot. Their quality can be Average or Poor, but all the bases in each battle group must have the same quality grading. Different battle groups can have different quality gradings. "German"-style infantry regiments can include Regimental Guns. These must be of the same quality grading as the battle group.

- Polish-style infantry regiments can only be used from 1673. They must be organised in battle groups of 6 bases. Their quality can be Average or Poor, but all the bases in each battle group must have the same quality grading. Different battle groups can have different quality gradings.

- From 1673 to 1679 both "German"-style and Polish-style infantry regiments can be used.

- The army must include at least 6 bases of "German"-style or Polish-style infantry regiments, which, date permitting, can be of either of these types. It cannot include more than 48 bases of both these types put together. Regimental Guns are markers, not bases, and do not count towards these totals.

- Medium artillery must be organised in battle groups of 2 bases.

- Light artillery can be organised in battle groups of 2, 3 or 4 bases. A 3 base battle group is allowed in this case because it is explicitly stated in the army list. If the list had "2-4" in the Bases per BG column, a battle group of 3 would not be allowed.

- All the bases in each Artillery battle group must be the same. Different Artillery battle groups can be different. The army cannot include more 2 bases of Medium Artillery, nor more than 4 bases of Light Artillery. It cannot include more than 4 bases of Artillery in total, and need not include any.

British Infantry

INDEX

References to illustrations are shown in **bold**.

Amexial, Battle of (1663) 42, 45

Anglo-Dutch naval wars 25, 52

Angus, Earl of 54

Argyll, Archibald, 8th Earl of 59

Argyll, Archibald, 9th Earl of 62

Aughrim, Battle of (1691) 79, 86, 87

Augsburg, War of the League of (1689–97)
   5, 19, 38, 47, 68–70, 77–79

Anglo-Dutch: Allies 83

   British Line Infantry **79**

   building a customised list 81–83

   Captain of the Earl of Angus' Regiment
      78

   Danish contingent 80

   Dragoon Officer **77**

   German contingent 80

   Hugeunot refugees 90

   Musketeer of Hasting's Regiment **78**

   Musketeer and Pikeman of King William's
      Army **84**

   Pikemen of the Earl of Argyll's Regiment
      78

   starter army 80

   Swedish contingent 80

   troop notes 79–80

Austria 6, 12, 25, 75

Azov 8

Bank of England 79

Bavaria, Elector of 48

bayonets: plug 4, 90

   socket 4, 29, 53

Bielke, Nils 22

Bothwell Bridge, Battle of (1679) 60

Boyne, Battle of the (1688) 77, 80, **81**,
   85–86, **88**

Brandenburg, Elector of 22

Brandenburg-Prussia 12, 21, 22, 25, 29, 37,
   38, 39

   infantryman **26**

British, Restoration: Allies 57

   building a customised list 56–57

   Cameronians 54

   Cavalry **45**, **55**, **63**

   Coldstream Regiment of Foot Guards **58**

   Dragoons 53, **53**

   Infantry 50, **98**

   Kings Royal Regiment of Foot Guards **51**

   King's Troop of Horse Guards **58**

   Lord Wentworth's Regiment of Foot Guards
      58

   Matchlockmen **52**, **64**

   Scots Greys 54

   starter army 54

   Tangiers Garrison **55**, **97**

   troop notes 53–54

Buchan, Maj-Gen Thomas 92

Candia, War of see Cretan War

Canea, Crete 18

Cannon, Maj-Gen Alexander 90

Cantanhede, Count of 45

Castel Rodrigo, Battle of (1664) 42, 45

Castelo Melhor, Count of 45

Catherine of Braganza, Princess 52

Catinat, General Nicolas 47

cavalry 5

Charles II, King of England 50–52, 59, 62

Charles II, King of Spain 42, 45

Christian IV, King of Denmark 28

Christian V, King of Denmark 29

Christina, Queen of Sweden 21

Churchill, John 79

Chyhyryn 7

Colbert, Jean Baptiste 66

Coligny-Saligny, Jean de 32

Condé, Louis II, Prince de 67, 68, 70

Copenhagen, siege of (1658) 22, 28

Cossacks 7, 12, 14, 96

Covenanting Rebels 54, **59**, 59–60

   building a customised list 61

   cavalry **60**

   starter army 61

   troop notes 60

Cretan War (1645–69) 18

Crete 18–19

Crimean Tatars 7–8, 11

Cromdale, Battle of (1690) 79, 92

Cromwell, Oliver 50

Dalmatia 18–19

Danish, later 28–29

   Austrian kürassiere 29, 34

   building a customised list 30–31

   Fynske Regiment infantryman **28**

   starter army 30

   troop notes 29

Dardanelles 19

D'Artagnan (Charles de Batz-Castelmore) 68

De Witt, Johan, Stadtholder 25

Denmark 12, 22

Derry, siege of (1689) 85, **86**

Devolution, War of (1666–67) 25, 66

Don River 8

Drumclog, Covenanter victory (1679) 59–60

Dumbarton's Regiment of Foot 5

Dundee, John Graham of Claverhouse, Viscount
   54, 59–60, 90

Dunkeld, Battle of (1689) 91–92

Dutch fleet 22, 28

Dutch, later 25

   Allies 28

   building a customised list 26–27

   Guards Infantry **25**

   Guards Officer **25**

   naval wars with England 25, 52

   starter army 26

Edict of Nantes 68

Elvas, Battle of (1659) 42, 45

Eugene of Savoy, Prince 33, 47

Fehrbellin, Battle of (1675) 22, 29, 39

Ferdinand III, Emperor 31

France 38

Franco-Dutch War (1672–78) 25, 32, 67–68

Frederick I, Elector of Brandenburg-Prussia
   39

Frederick III, King of Denmark 28, 29

Frederick William, Elector of Brandenburg-
   Prussia 12, 39

French, later Louis XIV 66–70

   Allies 74

   building a customised list 71–73

   Cavalryman of the Garde du Corps **69**

   Dragoons **73**

   Gardes Suisses **70**

   Grenadier à Cheval **69**

   Line Infantry **66**

   Musketeer of the Régiment des Gardes
      Françaises **69**

   Musketeers of the Régiments Furstenberg
      and Lyonnais **67**

   Pikeman of the Régiment Douglas **67**

   starter army 71

   troop notes 70–71

Genoese-Savoyard War 47

German States, later 37–39

   Allies 41

   Bavaria 37, 38

      starter army 39

   Brandenburg-Prussia 38, 39

   Braunschweig-Lunebergische Truppen **38**

   building a customised list 40–41

   Furst Leopold von Anhalt Dessau Regiment
      39

   Holy Roman Empire *Reichsarmee* 38

   Palatinate 38

   Saxony 37, 38, 39

Ginkell, Godert de 79

'Glorious Revolution' (1688) 50, 52, 59

Graham see Dundee, John Graham of
   Claverhouse, Viscount

Grand Alliance (1689–97) 47, 68

Grand Alliance, War of the see Augsburg,
   War of the League of (1689–97)

Halmstad, Battle of (1676) 22

Hapsburg Austrian Imperial 31–33

   Allies 37

   Austrian kürassiere 34

   building a customised list 35–36

   Polish Pancerni 34

   Sachsen-Koburg musketeer **32**

   starter army 34

   troop notes 33–34

Candia, War of see Cretan War